AWESOME
PAPER PLANES

Jeffrey Rutzky

"Neatly folded airplanes fly best. Your skills as a paper folder will increase with practice. Strive for perfection."

—Michael LaFosse, **Planes for Brains**

A QUIRK PACKAGING BOOK

©2010 by Quirk Packaging, Inc.

This book is part of the **Awesome Paper Planes** kit and is not to be sold separately.

Art directed by Lynne Yeamans
Book interior written, designed, and diagrammed by Jeffrey Rutzky
Symbols and Folding Techniques by Gay Merrill Gross
Edited by Tricia Levi
Photographed by Mark A. Gore

ISBN: 978-1-4351-2252-9

Printed and bound in China

10 9 8 7 6 5 4 3 2 1

The designs in this book are intended for personal use. Commercial use of any original model, in print or other media, requires the permission of the individual creator. The publishers have made every reasonable effort to contact the creators of the models herein. We apologize for any omissions and would be pleased to correct any such omissions in subsequent editions of this work.

Acknowledgments

Awesome Paper Planes, my fourth papercraft book, brings together a wide variety of models from many of the world's best paper airplane designers. Thank you to all of the creators who generously gave permission for the designs in this book.

Thanks again to Lynne Yeamans, whose art direction allows me to create beautiful work; Mark A. Gore, who professionally photographed the models I folded, as well as endured me as a "stylist"; and Tricia Levi for managing the project and for being a great editor and copilot. I am grateful to the ground crew at Quirk Packaging and to aviator Jennifer Boudinot, who folded the planes and made unscheduled landings among her coworkers' cubicles.

Once again, I am most indebted to Sharyn Rosart and Nathaniel Marunas for their support and encouragement—entrusting me to make papercraft books fly by sharing them with others.

Several paper engineers were helpful when I began to write and design this book: Stephen Weiss, Michael LaFosse, and Paul Jackson. Thanks to Nick Robinson, who taught me a new folding sequence for waterbomb-based planes. A special thank you to Sipho Mabona, who piloted me to other world-class designers. My wife, Nanci, continues to contribute to my publishing and production efforts, steering clear of my many test flights…and crashes! And finally I wish to thank Gay Merrill Gross, who taught me everything I know about origami instruction.

Dedicated to SSgt George W. Brown, USAF, ret.
From the Strategic Air Command to building
40-series model planes, George is still flying.

Contents

Introduction

"Paper airplanes are a fingertip expression of the freedom of flight."

—Stephen Weiss, **Wings & Things: Origami That Flies**

Awesome Paper Planes is a unique collection of paper airplane designs that brings together a wide variety of models from many of the world's best paper airplane designers. This kit also includes beautifully patterned sheets of paper that you can use to fold any of the models in the book.

If you want to practice folding the planes before using the patterned papers, simply use normal copier paper, either letter-size or trimmed to a square depending on the model.

History of Paper Flight

Many historians believe that Leonardo da Vinci invented the paper airplane—evidenced by his instructions for building a model plane from parchment. However, flying paper toys may have originated in China more than 2,000 years ago, when kites made from patterned paper and bamboo spars were popular.

The first modern paper airplanes are thought to have been created in 1930 by Jack Northrup, co-founder of Lockheed Corporation. Northrup made planes out of paper to help develop ideas for real aircraft.

Aerogami

Not surprisingly, paper airplanes are sometimes called aerogami, a term rooted in origami, the Japanese art of paper folding. Paper planes are called **kami hikoki** in Japanese; **kami** = paper, **hikoki** = airplane.

Folding paper planes is very popular because it's one of the easiest ways for beginner origami-makers to master basic folding techniques. The ubiquitous Classic Dart can be made in only five steps!

Darts, Gliders, and Stunts

The models in this book have been divided into three categories.

Darts are mostly thrown hard—and fly fast and straight. But be careful with the pointy ones! The tips are sharp. Some darts, like the Falcon or Nike (pages 45 and 52), are more delicate, designed to resemble real aircraft.

Gliders are generally designed to fly smoothly, steadily, and for a long time—the current indoor record is nearly 30 seconds! Outdoors, some gliders will even fly away, continually lifted on thermals or simply carried away by the wind. Competition winners in the Time Aloft category are always gliders. Gliders, however, can also be made to perform stunts.

Stunts can be predictable—designed to fly in a loop right back to your hand. Their unpredictability can be fun, too. The Astro Tube or Crazy Stunter (pages 106 and 108) can spin or loop in a different direction each time you throw them.

To Fold, or To Cut and Glue

Other paper airplane books or kits feature models designed to be carefully cut out, assembled, and glued together. Some of these designs may be impressive to look at and fly very well, too. But there's no substitute for folding a simple sheet of paper into a fun-to-fly toy, and knowing that if it becomes damaged or stuck in a tree, you can easily fold another one.

Familiarize, Fold, and Fly

Before you begin folding, take a few minutes to familiarize yourself with the Airplane Parts, Paper Plane Parts, and Trim Tips (pages 8–10). You should also follow the basic guidelines in each model's Flight Plan. Most paper airplanes won't fly their best until they've been tested and trimmed. However, if the planes have been carefully and symmetrically folded, some of them won't require any trimming.

Once you're acquainted with the basics, it's time to fill your hangar with this cool collection of colorful aircraft!

"A rectangle of paper is the low end of technology when it comes to flight. It is figuratively and literally the thinnest possible technological barrier between us and the air."
—John M. Collins, **The Gliding Flight**

Airplane Parts

Most aircraft, from large airliners and fighter jets to small aircraft and even radio-controlled model planes, have similar parts. If you've observed a commercial jet at the gate of an airport, you may have noticed flaps on the wings and stabilizer, or seen its tail fin with the rudder turned. These relatively small surfaces have a huge impact on how the plane flies.

A typical airplane is pictured below. It has the same features as many of the planes you'll fold. However, you'll have to make your own elevons (also called elevators) and rudders—the two most important trim surfaces on a paper airplane.

The pilot of a real airplane has a greater variety of surfaces to use to maintain control while the plane is flying—but the principles are the same. Pilots use a combination of the wings' ailerons and the tail fin's rudder to turn and bank, and a combination of the stabilizers' elevators and the engines' thrust to climb.

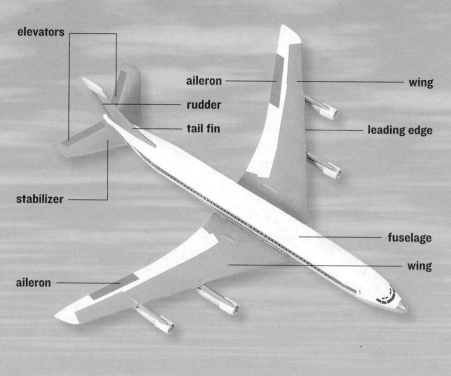

elevators
aileron — wing
rudder
tail fin — leading edge
stabilizer
fuselage
aileron — wing

Paper Plane Parts

Although the paper planes come in many shapes, all the basic parts you will encounter in this book have been labeled in the illustration below.

You may not find every trim surface on every plane, but all of the models have some way of correcting their flight paths.

The elevon flaps you can make combine the functions of a real plane's elevator and aileron. Some models have winglets that help control how straight the plane flies.

Paper airplane pilots use a combination of the wings' elevons and rudder to fly straight or turn, and a combination of the wings' elevons and throwing speed to climb or glide smoothly.

Stunt flying requires exaggerated control over the elevons and rudder to make the plane loop, swoop, or even return back to your hand!

Depending on the model, very small adjustments can make a big difference in how the plane flies.

"As an engineer in the aviation industry, my paper airplane designs tend to be heavily influenced by my desire for better aerodynamics, structure, and performance."

—Teong Hin Tan, **Interlocking and 3D Paper Airplanes**

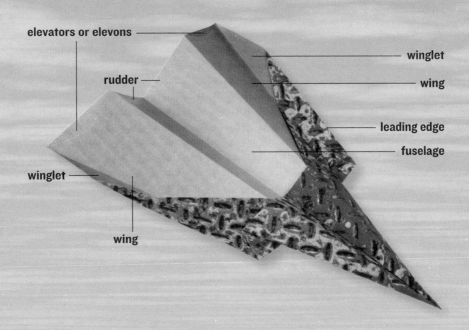

elevators or elevons

rudder

winglet

wing

winglet

wing

leading edge

fuselage

Flight Plan

Each plane has a Flight Plan—a guideline for the wings' dihedral angle, and trim tips that may be unique to that plane's design and will help it fly. Follow these tips to maximize the success of each design.

Flight Plan

Check to make sure the wings are aligned as shown above.

Trim Tips

The following section contains the most important information on how to get your planes to fly.

Although not a complete lesson in aerodynamics, it will give you the basics. Trimming using the control surfaces—in conjunction with the Flight Plan the creator often recommends for his design—can help make the plane fly better.

Neatness Counts. A Lot!

Fold with as much accuracy as possible, since a balanced plane depends on good symmetry. It may be easier to learn how to fold some of the planes if you practice on letter-size paper.

Have Patience!

Even if you've folded your plane perfectly, there's no guarantee it will fly well the first time you launch it. Don't give up! There are myriad reasons it might not fly well, such as launch speed or wing angles.

Pitch, Roll, and Yaw

In pilot lingo, **pitch** means climb or dive; **roll** means spinning around the fuselage's axis; and **yaw** means turning left or right.

pitch   roll   yaw

Dihedral Angle

This is the angle of the wings to the fuselage. Each Flight Plan profiles the wings when the plane is at rest.

Making Adjustments

To fix flight problems, begin with the dihedral angle: Make sure it matches the Flight Plan diagram. This can have a major impact on performance.

Slightly curve the back edges (elevons) of the wings up or down to correct pitch—when the plane climbs, stalls, dives, or just dive-bombs to the ground.

Slightly curve the back edges (rudder) of the fuselage to correct yaw—when the plane turns sharply to the left or right.

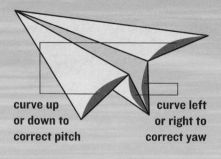

curve up or down to correct pitch   curve left or right to correct yaw

Origami Basics

Fold Lines
Familiarize yourself with these Fold Lines, which are similar to the conventions used in origami diagramming.

Mountain Fold

Mountain Crease

Valley Fold

Valley Crease

Valley Fold
Fold on this line to create a groove or valley.

- - - - - - - - - - - - - - - - - -

Mountain Fold
Fold on this line to create a peak or ridge.

Crease
A thin line indicates a crease after a fold has been unfolded.

X-ray View
A dotted line indicates either a hidden edge or an imaginary reference line.

Arrows & Other Symbols

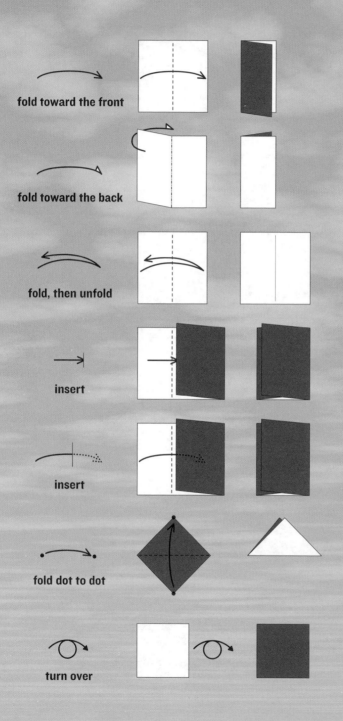

fold toward the front

fold toward the back

fold, then unfold

insert

insert

fold dot to dot

turn over

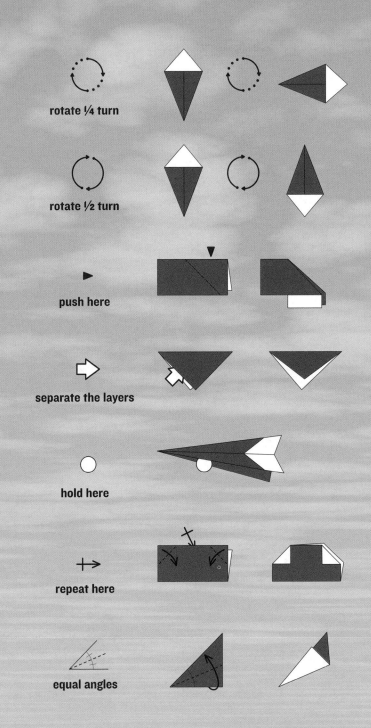

rotate ¼ turn

rotate ½ turn

push here

separate the layers

hold here

repeat here

equal angles

Folding Techniques

Inside Reverse Fold
An end tucks inside, between layers.

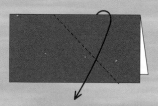

1 Precrease.

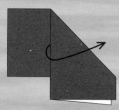

2 Crease sharply, and unfold.

3 Partially unfold.

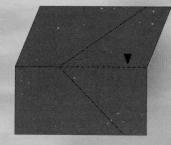

4 Reverse two creases.

5 Push in between the layers.

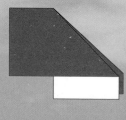

6 Flatten the finished Inside Reverse Fold.

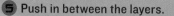

Outside Reverse Fold
An end wraps around the layers.

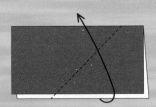

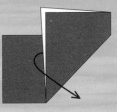

1 Precrease.

2 Crease sharply, and unfold.

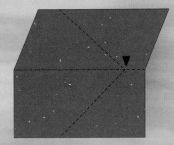

3 Partially unfold.

4 Press at the intersection point and reverse two creases.

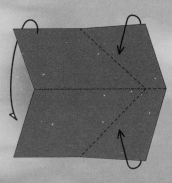

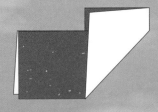

5 Collapse along the creases.

6 Flatten the finished Outside Reverse Fold.

Squash Fold

A double layer flap is opened and squashed flat.

1 Precrease, and unfold.

2 Raise the flap.

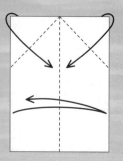

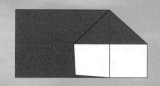

3 Pull apart the layers; press the folded edge, squashing...

4 ...flat and symmetrical.

Airplane Fold

The beginning fold of many paper airplanes, including the Classic Dart. Make this fold precisely since it sets the airplane's initial symmetry.

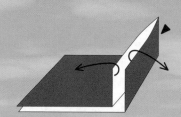

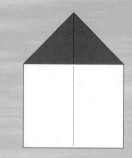

1 White side up, fold in half long edge to long edge, and unfold. Fold down the top corners to the center crease.

2 The finished Airplane Fold. This fold may also be made horizontally, folding short edge to short edge first.

Rabbit Ear Fold

A Rabbit Ear Fold is a technique where two adjacent edges are folded in together, squashing a flap that looks like a pointed rabbit ear. Practice on a small square of scrap paper.

1 Fold in half, corner to opposite corner, and unfold. Repeat in the other direction.

2 Fold a lower edge to the horizontal crease, but crease only from the side corner to the vertical centerline, and unfold.

3 Repeat step **2** on the right edge.

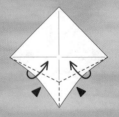

4 Rabbit Ear Fold: Refold on three existing creases; the bottom corner will protrude upward forming a...

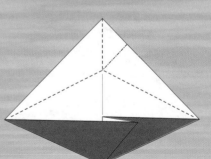

5 ..."rabbit ear." Flatten this new flap to the right.

6 The finished Rabbit Ear Fold. A typical diagram for a Rabbit Ear Fold is pictured on the top half.

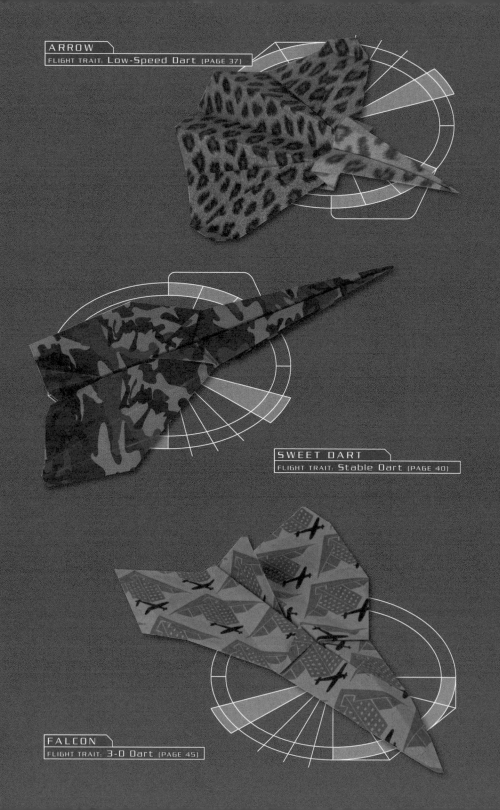

ARROW
FLIGHT TRAIT: Low-Speed Dart (PAGE 37)

SWEET DART
FLIGHT TRAIT: Stable Dart (PAGE 40)

FALCON
FLIGHT TRAIT: 3-D Dart (PAGE 45)

DARTS

"Darts. These are muscle planes."
—John M. Collins, **The Gliding Flight**

Darts are designed to achieve maximum speed and distance.
Unlike gliders, they do not stay aloft for a long time, unless
launched from the window of a skyscraper! The Classic Dart,
Dragon, and Cruise Missile are designed to travel far and fast.
They fly well outside because they are simple and durable.
The Falcon, Crow, and Nike darts are designed to look like
real fighter jets. These models are best flown gently indoors,
or outside on a calm day.

Classic Dart

The Classic Dart
is the most ubiquitous paper
airplane ever made. No one knows
when the design first appeared—was
this the legendary design da Vinci
is credited with? This version, from
a family of darts, is the easiest to
make and fly—it's likely you already
know how. As a safety reminder:
keep everyone, including pets, away
from the pointy end!

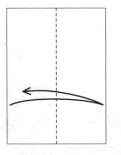

1 White side up, fold in half long
edge to long edge. Crease, and
unfold.

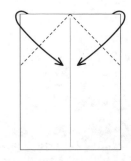

2 Fold down the top corners to
the center crease. This completes
the Airplane Fold (page 16).

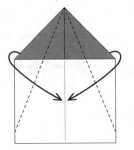

3 Fold the upper sloping edges to the center crease.

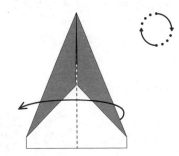

4 Valley-fold the plane in half. Rotate ¼-turn clockwise.

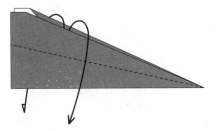

5 Fold both wings in half.

6 The finished Classic Dart. ■

Flight Plan

Adjust the wings to match the dihedral angle shown above.

Hold the fuselage in the middle and throw hard. If the Classic Dart nose dives, try throwing at an upward angle, or adjust the elevons up a little. If it turns, adjust the rudder slightly. This model flies best outdoors or in a large indoor space.

Dragon

The versatile Dragon, with its heavy nose and puffy wings, can glide for long distances and even fly stunts. Designer Alex Schultz notes that the Dragon is also "the best plane for trying to hit your teacher with"—but don't blame us if you get detention!

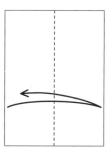

1 White side up, fold in half long edge to long edge. Crease, and unfold.

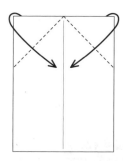

2 Fold down the top corners to the center crease. This completes the Airplane Fold (page 16).

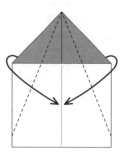

3 Fold the upper sloping edges to the center crease.

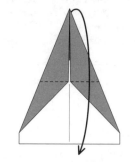

4 Fold down the top point, keeping the center creases aligned.

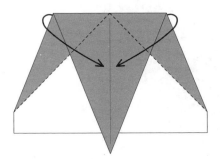

5 Airplane-fold the top edges to the center crease.

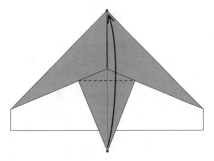

6 Fold up the bottom point to meet the top point.

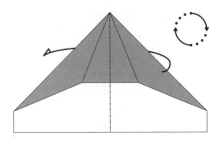

7 Mountain-fold the plane in half. Rotate ¼-turn clockwise.

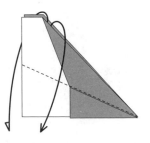

8 Fold both wings in half.

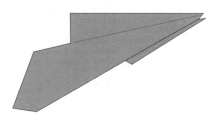

9 The finished Dragon. ■

Flight Plan

Adjust the wings to match the dihedral angle shown above.

Hold the fuselage about a third of the way from the nose and throw hard. If the Dragon nose dives, try throwing at a slight upward angle, or adjust the elevons up a little. If it turns, adjust the rudder slightly. This model flies well indoors or out.

Interceptor

This sleek dart by Stephen Weiss travels straight and can maintain a horizontal flight, even when landing. Large winglets and a tail fin add to its stability. Like most of Weiss' planes, there's no need for trimming if you fold it accurately and symmetrically.

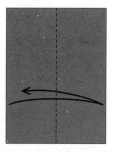

1 Colored side up, fold in half long edge to long edge. Crease, and unfold.

2 Fold down the top corners to the center crease.

3 Turn over.

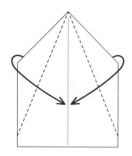

4 Fold the upper sloping edges to the center crease.

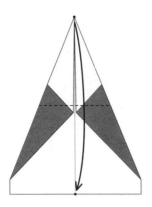

5 Fold down the top point to meet the bottom edge.

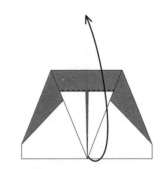

6 Fold up the bottom point along the horizontal raw edges shown.

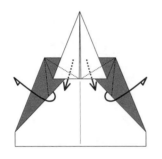

7 Swivel the sloping raw edge flap on each side out so that it pulls the flap underneath making the hidden Valley Fold and the Mountain Fold shown.

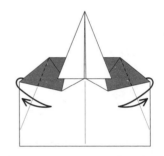

8 Fold both winglets on the existing creases. Crease, and unfold.

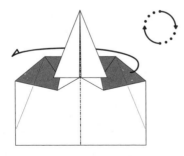

9 Mountain-fold the plane in half. Rotate ¼-turn clockwise.

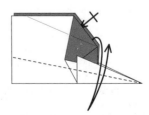

10 Fold down the wing, bisecting the nose. Crease, and unfold. Repeat with the other wing.

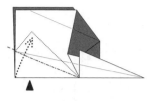

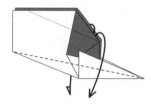

11 Inside-reverse-fold (page 14) the tail fin between the wings on the angle shown.

12 Fold down both wings on the existing creases.

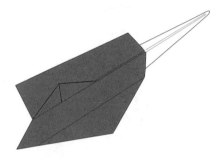

13 Fold the tail fin on the angle shown, tucking it into the fuselage as far as possible. Unfold the wings and adjust the winglets to match the Flight Plan.

14 The finished Interceptor. ■

Flight Plan

Adjust the wings and winglets to match the dihedral angle shown above.

Hold the fuselage in the middle and throw moderately hard. The Interceptor flies straight and maintains its course. If it takes a nose dive, try throwing at a slight upward angle, or adjust the elevons up a little. If it turns, adjust the tail fin slightly. This model flies well indoors or out.

Needle Dart

The **Needle Dart** features an enormous wing area, balanced by its concentrated nose weight. Its stability makes it ideal for hard-throwing outdoor flight. Nick Robinson's complex design reveals his extraordinary skills as an origami model designer.

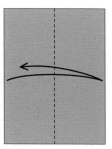

1 Colored side up, fold in half long edge to long edge, and unfold.

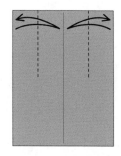

2 Bring the long edge to the center crease and fold only about halfway. Crease lightly, and unfold.

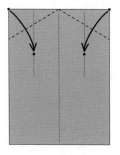

3 Fold the top corners to the creases made in Step **2**.

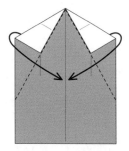

4 Airplane-fold (page 16) the upper sloping edges to the center crease.

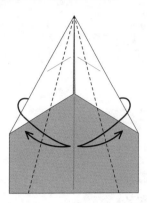

5 Fold the upper sloping edges to the center crease. Crease, and unfold.

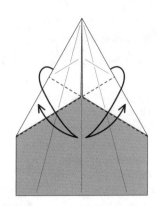

6 Fold the upper sloping edges in half on the angle shown. Crease, and unfold.

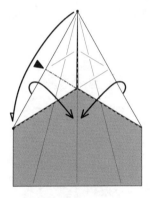

7 Rabbit Ear Fold (page 17): Collapse the side triangles on the existing creases with the "ear" pointing left.

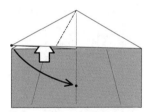

8 Separate the layers and squash-fold the "rabbit ear" aligning with the center crease.

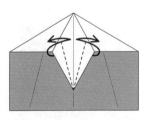

9 Fold the lower sloping edges to the center crease. Crease, and unfold.

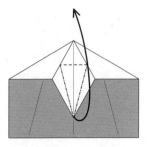

10 Fold the bottom point up, reversing the front creases made in Step **9**.

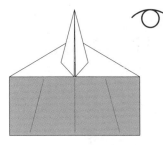

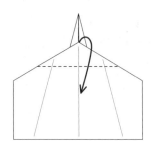

11 Turn over.

12 Fold down the point using the existing hidden horizontal crease as a guide.

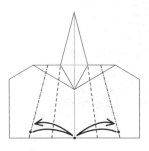

13 Using the existing Mountain Folds as a guide, valley-fold each wing on the angle shown. Crease, and unfold.

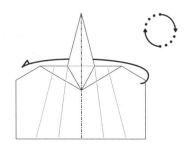

14 Mountain-fold the plane in half. Rotate ¼-turn clockwise.

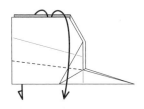

15 Fold down both wings.

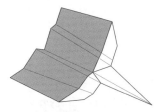

16 The finished Needle Dart. Follow the Flight Plan to adjust the wings and winglets. ■

Flight Plan

Adjust the wings to match the dihedral angle shown above.

Hold the fuselage in the middle and throw hard. If the Needle Dart takes a nose dive, try throwing at a slight upward angle, or adjust the elevons up a little. If it turns, adjust the rudder slightly. This model flies well indoors or out.

Prize Winner

Sleek and unique with its inside-out look, this fast flier has a thin, sharp nose that slices through the air. Its design, winner of the origami category in the historic First International Paper Airplane Competition, was created by the late James Sakoda, a prolific designer of origami models.

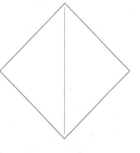

1 Begin with a square, white side up, creased along one diagonal.

2 Fold the lower sloping edges inward to meet at the center crease.

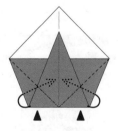

3 Fold the bottom point up to the point marked.

4 Inside-reverse-fold (page 14) the lower corners underneath the top flap.

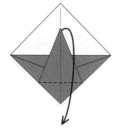

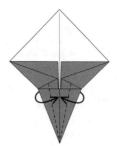

5 Fold down the top layer's triangular point.

6 Fold the top layer's lower sloping edges to the center.

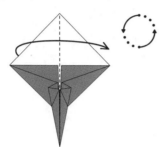

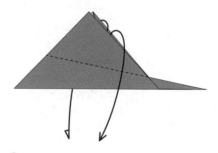

7 Fold in half. Rotate ¼-turn counterclockwise.

8 Fold down the wings, extending the angle of the nose as shown.

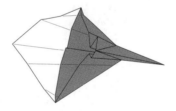

9 Fold up the winglets on the angle shown.

10 The finished Prize Winner. Follow the Flight Plan to adjust the wings and winglets. ■

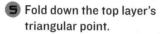

Flight Plan

Adjust the wings and winglets to match the dihedral angle shown above.

Throw with a moderate speed at first to see if trimming is required. If the Prize Winner flies straight, try throwing high up in the air with a hard launch; it will glide down smoothly. You can fly this model inside or out.

Greatest YZ

Named after flying a record of over 500 feet (150 m) in ten minutes, catching thermals along the way, "Wisey" was the envy of the schoolyard! A variation of the Classic Dart design, it comes from brothers Allan and David Wise of Australia, who created it when they were kids. Winglets and a stronger fuselage make this plane great for outside launches, especially from a high point.

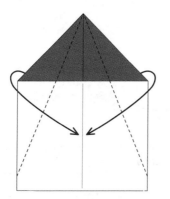

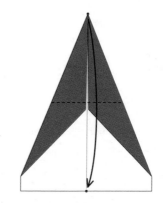

1 Begin with the Airplane Fold (page 16). Fold the upper sloping edges to the center crease.

2 Fold down the top point to meet the bottom edge.

3 Fold up the bottom point along the hidden horizontal raw edges.

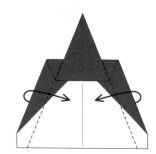

4 Fold in both winglets on the angle shown.

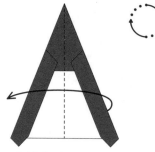

5 Valley-fold the plane in half. Rotate ¼-turn clockwise.

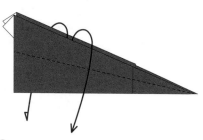

6 Fold both wings in half.

7 The finished Greatest YZ. Follow the Flight Plan to adjust the wings and winglets. ■

Flight Plan

Adjust the wings to match the dihedral angle shown above.

Hold the fuselage in the middle and throw hard. The Greatest YZ flies best outdoors, especially if there are medium winds and thermals.

Swooping Hawk

Two planes in one: Just like the bird it's named after, the Swooping Hawk has a streamlined, compact shape that allows it to fly straight and fast like a dart—but it can glide, too. Stephen Weiss added versatility, designing a plane that soars when its wings are spread out and it is launched gently.

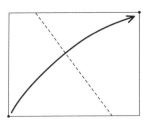

1 White side up, fold lower left corner to upper right corner.

2 Arrange the paper so the fold is horizontal as shown. Fold up the bottom edge.

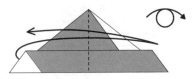

3 Fold in half. Crease, and unfold. Turn over.

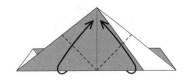

4 Fold the bottom edges to the center crease.

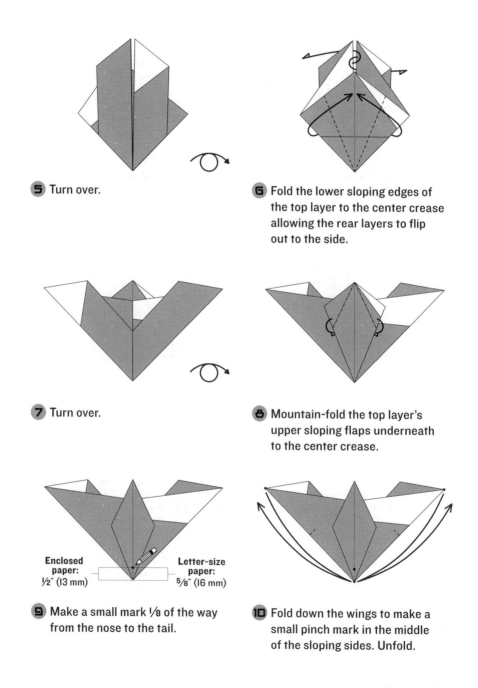

5 Turn over.

6 Fold the lower sloping edges of the top layer to the center crease allowing the rear layers to flip out to the side.

7 Turn over.

8 Mountain-fold the top layer's upper sloping flaps underneath to the center crease.

Enclosed paper: ½″ (13 mm)

Letter-size paper: ⅝″ (16 mm)

9 Make a small mark ⅛ of the way from the nose to the tail.

10 Fold down the wings to make a small pinch mark in the middle of the sloping sides. Unfold.

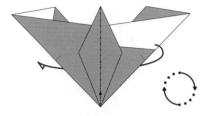

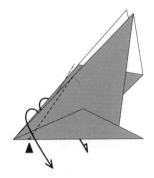

11 Mountain-fold the plane in half. Rotate ¼-turn clockwise.

12 Outside-reverse-fold (page 15) the "head" using the reference marks made in Steps **9–10**.

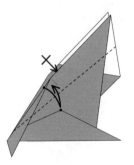

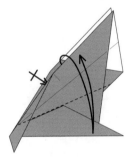

13 Fold down each winglet, matching the leading edge with the body's sloping edge. Crease, and unfold.

14 Fold down each wing on the angle shown. Crease, and unfold.

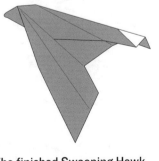

15 The finished Swooping Hawk. Follow the Flight Plan to adjust the wings and winglets. ■

Flight Plan

Adjust the wings and winglets to match the dihedral angle shown above.

Hold the Swooping Hawk by the body and throw with a moderate to hard speed. Vary the launch angle and speed for best flight. Also try a launch similar to that of the Flying Wing: Flatten the wings somewhat and hold the tail end with your index finger inside the body and your thumb and middle finger gripping the bottom. Release gently.

Arrow

With its sleek, graceful design, this plane may look like a dart but it flies slower than most, much more like a glider. By using the diagonal of the square as a starting point, the Arrow has more directional stability—and that means straighter flights. This is just the effect designer Sipho Mabona was after.

1 Begin with a square, colored side up, creased along one diagonal.

2 Fold in the upper sloping edges to meet at the center crease.

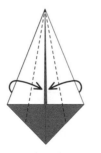

3 Again, fold in the upper sloping edges to meet at the center crease.

4 Fold the lower sloping edge to align with the upper sloping edge. Make a small pinch mark, and unfold.

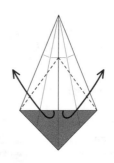

5 Fold down the top point to the pinch mark made in Step **4**. Crease, and unfold. Unfold the top flaps back to Step **3**.

6 Fold the top flaps out at the angle shown, starting at the crease made in Step **5**.

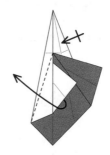

7 Fold the left side back in on the existing crease.

8 Fold the left top flaps out at the angle shown, starting at the crease made in Step **5**. Repeat Steps **7–8** with the right side.

9 Fold the left side back in on the existing crease.

10 Fold the right corner of the top flap to the creaseline on the angle shown. Then fold back out on the crease made in Step **8**. Repeat Steps **9–10** with the right side.

11 Fold down the top point at the base of the tiny white triangles.

12 Fold up the bottom point on the existing creases.

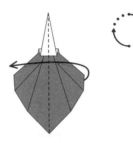

13 Valley-fold the plane in half. Rotate ¼-turn clockwise.

14 Mountain-fold the winglet parallel to the outside edge. Fold down the wing, bisecting the fuselage but not the nose. Repeat with the other wing.

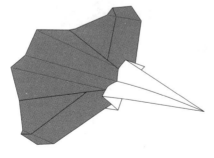

15 The finished Arrow. Follow the Flight Plan to adjust the wings and winglets. ▣

Flight Plan

Adjust the wings and winglets to the dihedral angle shown above.

The Arrow depends on the right balance to fly well. Hold the fuselage in the center and launch this model with a gentle toss. It flies well from a platform above ground level and will glide straight. Fly the Arrow indoors to determine if any trim is required. For best results, fly this plane outdoors on a calm day.

Sweet Dart

An innovative locked-fuselage design makes the **Sweet Dart** an especially reliable and durable flier. Invented by **Michael LaFosse**, a leading paper airplane designer, origami expert, and papermaker, this technique allows the wing's dihedral to remain as set— so the plane flies without wobbling through the air. Added flight stabilizers: Adjustable built-in elevons.

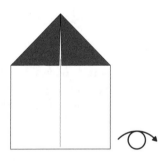

1 Begin with the Airplane Fold (page 16). Turn over.

2 Fold down the top point to the bottom edge.

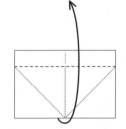

3 Turn over.

4 Fold up the top layer along the hidden raw edges underneath.

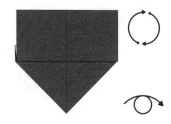

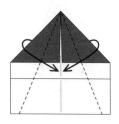

5 Turn over. Rotate ½-turn.

6 Airplane-fold the upper sloping edges to the center crease.

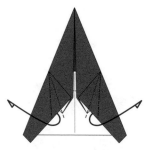

7 Swivel the top-layer flap of each wing out as far as it will go. Squash-fold (page 16) the resulting creases.

8 Fold the lower edges of the wings underneath the hidden flap. Begin at the center and end at the existing crease.

9 Fold in the winglets so the vertical raw edge aligns with the existing crease as shown.

10 Turn over.

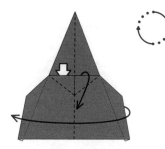
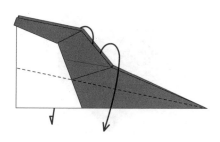

11 Create the fuselage lock by lifting up the small pocket as far as it will go while folding the plane in half. Rotate ¼-turn clockwise.

12 Fold down both wings, bisecting the fuselage on the angle shown.

13 Fold the top layer of the tail so the raw edge aligns with the existing crease. Repeat on the other side.

14 Squash-fold the flap so the right edge aligns with the crease made in Step 13. Repeat with the other side. Flatten all folds back to Step 13.

15 The finished Sweet Dart. Follow the Flight Plan to adjust the wings and winglets. ■

Flight Plan

Adjust the wings and winglets to match the dihedral angle shown above.

This plane is perfect for moderate to hard throws outdoors on windy or calm days. For long-duration flights, throw upward. Trim the built-in elevons for added lift. LaFosse suggests making one without the elevons in Steps 13–14 for faster flights.

Cruise Missile

A locked-fuselage design holds this plane together, resulting in superior structure and enhanced aerodynamic performance. A blunt nose that isn't easily damaged increases this plane's durability, too. Teong Hin Tan's Cruise Missile is a smart-looking, simple dart that will fly fast and straight.

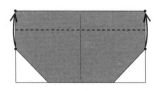

1 Begin with the Airplane Fold (page 16). Fold down the top point to the bottom edges of the flaps.

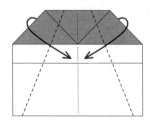

2 Fold down the top edge to the bottom edge.

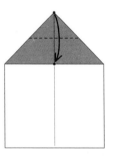

3 Fold up the top layer so the side points align as shown.

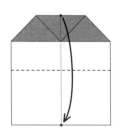

4 Fold the sloping side edges to the center crease.

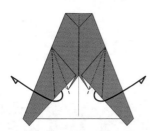

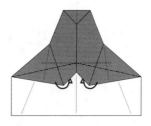

5 Swivel the top-layer flap of each wing out as far as it will go. Squash-fold (page 16) the resulting creases.

6 Fold the lower edges of the wings underneath the hidden flap. Begin at the center and end at the outer corner.

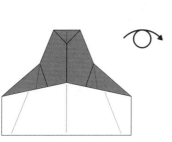

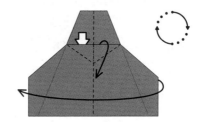

7 Turn over.

8 Create the fuselage lock by lifting up the small pocket as far as it will go while folding the plane in half. Rotate ¼-turn clockwise.

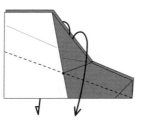

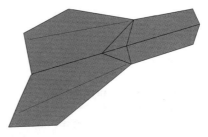

9 Fold down both wings, starting at the bottom of the nose and going through the point marked.

Flight Plan

Adjust the wings to the slight dihedral angle shown above.

This plane is perfect for moderate to hard throws outdoors on windy or calm days. For long-duration flights, throw upward. Trim the elevons for added lift. Because of the locked-fuselage design, the Cruise Missile makes a very reliable and durable flier, and if it hits the wall, the nose isn't easily damaged.

10 The finished Cruise Missile. Follow the Flight Plan to adjust the wings. ∎

Falcon

With its 3-D fuselage and fuselage lock, two features that reduce drag and increase aero-dynamics, this plane is ready for action. Measure carefully as you make it—a ruler is key—so that this ultra-cool fighter jet is as balanced and symmetrical as possible. It's another Teong Hin Tan–designed model that's lots of fun to fold and fly.

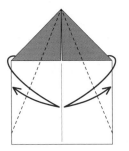

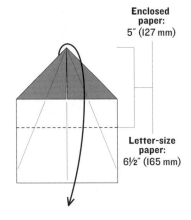

Enclosed paper:
5″ (127 mm)

Letter-size paper:
6½″ (165 mm)

1 Begin with the Airplane Fold (page 16). Fold the upper sloping edges to the center crease. Crease, and unfold.

2 Fold down the top point on the horizontal line as shown.

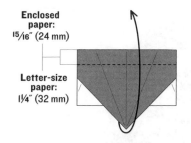

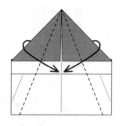

3 Fold up the bottom point on the horizontal line as shown.

4 Airplane-fold the upper sloping edges to the center using the existing creases.

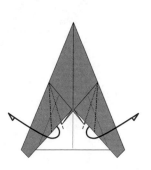

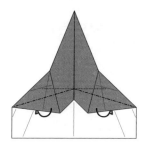

5 Swivel the top-layer flap of each wing out as far as it will go. Squash-fold (page 16) the resulting creases.

6 Fold the lower edges of the wings underneath the hidden flap. Begin at the center and end at the existing crease.

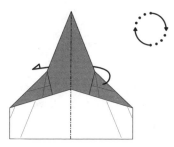

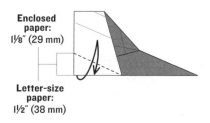

7 Mountain-fold the plane in half. Rotate ¼-turn clockwise.

8 Fold up the tail fin at the angle shown. Crease, and unfold.

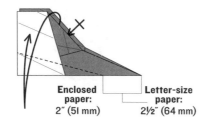

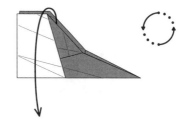

9 Fold down the wing on the angle shown. The nose will twist upward. Crease, and unfold. Repeat on the other side.

10 Unfold along the center crease and rotate ¼-turn counterclockwise.

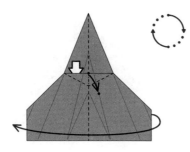

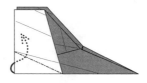

11 Create the fuselage lock: Place the center point on the crease made in Step **9** by liting up the small pocket. Valley-fold the plane in half, squashing the lock in place. Rotate ¼-turn clockwise.

12 Inside-reverse-fold (page 14) the tail fin up on the existing creases made in Step **8**.

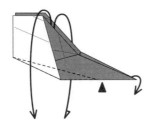

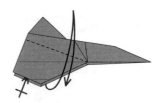

13 Fold down the wings on the existing creases made in Step **9**. Carefully flip the nose so it points down when both wings are folded.

14 Fold up the wings at the angle shown. Crease, and unfold. Repeat on the other side, matching the edges carefully.

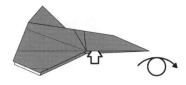

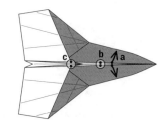

15 Open up the plane and turn it upside down as shown in Step **16**.

16 Make the fuselage 3-D:
   a. Pull down the outermost layers.
   b. Pinch together to hold sides...
   c. ...and squash excess paper together to lock.

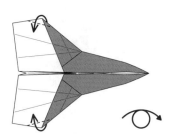

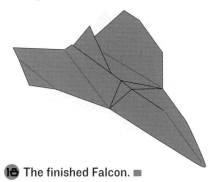

17 Fold up the winglets at a 90-degree angle to the wing. Turn over. Follow the Flight Plan to adjust the wings.

18 The finished Falcon. ▪

Flight Plan

Adjust the wings and winglets to match the dihedral angle shown above.
   Hold the fuselage in the middle and throw with moderate force—indoors or, if there are calm winds, outdoors. For longer-duration flights, throw upward. Trim the elevons for added lift or the tail fin to correct turns. If the 3-D fuselage pops back in, put a tiny drop of glue at position "b" in Step **16**.

Crow

Realistic air intakes are a unique feature of this detail-packed plane. Careful folding to make the Crow perfectly symmetrical will enhance the balance it needs for flight. This is one of Thay Yang's military aircraft designs, among a fleet of more challenging paper planes to fold and fly.

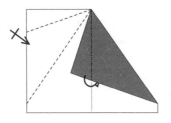

1 White side up, fold in half short edge to short edge, and unfold.

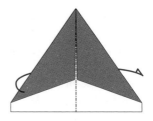

Enclosed paper: ½" (13 mm)

Letter-size paper: ¾" (19 mm)

2 Fold the upper right corner past the center crease on the angle shown.

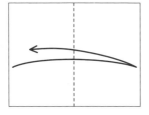

3 Mountain-fold the corner aligning the fold with the center crease. Repeat Steps **2–3** on the left.

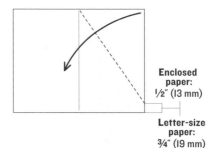

4 Mountain-fold the left side behind the right side.

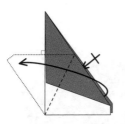

5 Fold up the top layer so the folded edge makes a right angle to the center fold as shown. Repeat on the other side.

6 Fold down the top layer so the folded edge makes a right angle to the lower sloping edge as shown. Repeat on the other side.

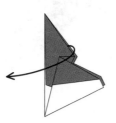

7 Open up the model as shown in Step **8**.

8 Fold the upper sloping edges toward the center crease as far as you can on the angle shown.

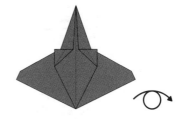

9 Open up the side "air intakes" and squash-fold so the top edge is perpendicular to the center crease.

10 Turn over.

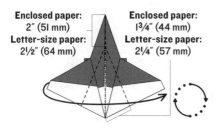

Enclosed paper:
2″ (51 mm)
Letter-size paper:
2½″ (64 mm)

Enclosed paper:
1¾″ (44 mm)
Letter-size paper:
2¼″ (57 mm)

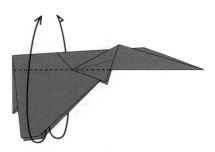

11 Precrease the diagonal folds. Fold in half on the existing creases. Rotate ¼-turn clockwise.

12 Fold up the wings using the bottom front of the fuselage as your guide.

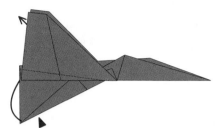

13 Inside-reverse-fold (page 14) the tail along the hidden line shown.

14 Fold down the winglets so the raw edges align. Repeat on the other side.

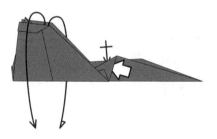

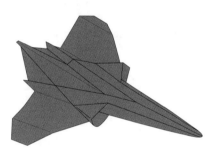

15 Bring down the wings and insert your thumb into the intake ports to round them out.

16 The finished Crow. Fold the winglets at a 90-degree angle to the wing. Follow the Flight Plan to adjust the wings. ▪

Flight Plan

Adjust the wings, winglets, and tail fin to match the dihedral angle shown above.

Hold the plane midway inside the fuselage. Throw with a gentle to moderate speed. The Crow is best flown indoors. Trimming of the tail fin may be necessary to get it to fly straight. Bend the elevons up slightly if it takes a nose dive.

TFB-1 "Nike"
with Display Stand

A delta-winged fighter look-alike, the **TFB-1 "Nike"** has an aerodynamic form and is a remarkable flier—like the real thing. Designer Marvin Goody has created a number of origami models, but this one is a standout. Attach the plane to its integrated base so even when this aircraft is parked at your desk, it looks like it's ready for action.

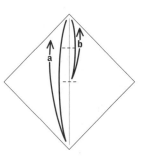

1 Begin with a square, white side up, creased along one diagonal.
a. Fold the top corner to the bottom corner to make a pinch mark, and unfold.
b. Fold the top corner to the center pinch mark to make another pinch mark, and unfold.

2 Fold the bottom corner to the ¼ pinch mark made in Step **1b.**

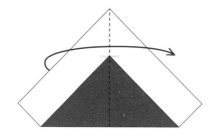

3 Fold in half on the existing vertical crease.

4 Fold up the top flap so the bottom folded edge aligns with the left side folded edge. Repeat on the other side.

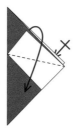

5 Fold down the top layer's upper point on the angle shown. Repeat on the other side.

6 Fold up the top layer's bottom point so the raw edge aligns with the upper folded edge. Repeat on the other side.

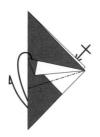

7 Mountain-fold the top layer's upper edge behind so it aligns with the lower folded edge. Crease, and unfold. Repeat on the other side.

8 Reach inside the large triangle and while holding the upper part where shown, pull down the tip of the square inside all of the way. The side flaps will unfold, too.

9 Make two new pinch marks by folding the top point down to each end of the existing creaseline and unfolding.

10 Fold from the original center pinch mark made in Step **1** so the left edge aligns with the pinch mark on the right sloping edge.

11 Fold the top point back from the pinch mark made in Step **9** on the angle shown.

12 Unfold Steps **10–11**. Reverse the top layer's folds so the upper triangle sinks in between the folds made in Step **10**.

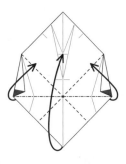

13 Open up the model along the center crease.

14 Collapse the bottom point along the existing creases.

15 Fold the top flaps' upper sloping edges to the center. Crease, and unfold.

16 Bring down the top layer only, reversing two Valley Folds. Fold all raw edges on existing creases to meet at the center.

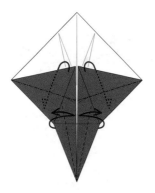

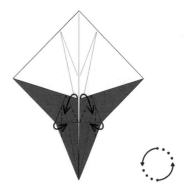

17 Fold the top layer's lower sloping edges to the center. Crease, and unfold. Mountain-fold the flaps inside the model on the existing creases.

18 Fold in the top layer's side points to lie on the intersection of the existing creases. Fold the inner corners down as shown. Rotate ¼-turn counterclockwise.

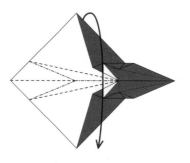

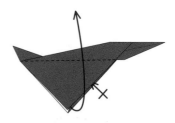

19 Fold the model in half. Take care that the tail fin sinks back into the existing creases shown.

20 Fold up the wing on the angle shown. Repeat on the other side.

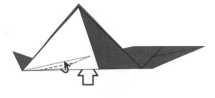

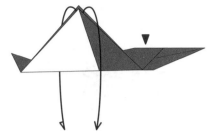

21 Reach in between the rear of the fuselage and carefully fold over the tail fin's hidden flap to lock.

22 Fold the wings back down and squash the "cockpit" area a little to round out the fuselage.

23 The finished TFB-1 "Nike." Follow the Flight Plan to adjust the wings. Then make a Display Stand for your jet. ▪

Flight Plan

Adjust the wings to the dihedral angle shown above.

The secret to flying this plane is in its launch. Hold the nose just ahead of the wings and launch with a gentle, straight toss. Another method the creator suggests is to hold the leading edge of either wing and throw high into the air. It will climb and then smoothly glide back down.

Display Stand for "Nike"

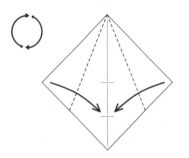

1 Complete Step 1 of the "Nike" on page 52. Rotate ½-turn. Fold in the upper sloping edges to meet at the center crease.

2 Fold up the lower sloping edges using the side corners and the ¼ pinch mark as a guide. Crease, and unfold.

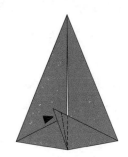

3 Rabbit Ear Fold (page 17): Bring the lower sloping edges back up on the existing creases; flatten the excess paper to the left and right.

4 Squash-fold (page 16) the "rabbit ear" so its center aligns with the main center crease.

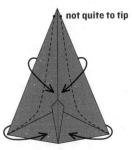

not quite to tip

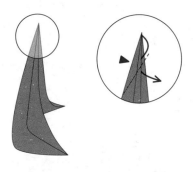

5 Make folds along lines shown. Curve bottom of stand into a horseshoe shape.

6 Inside-reverse-fold (page 14) the tip. You may need to practice a few times to get the angle you want.

7 The finished Display Stand for "Nike." Insert tip into pocket under plane. ■

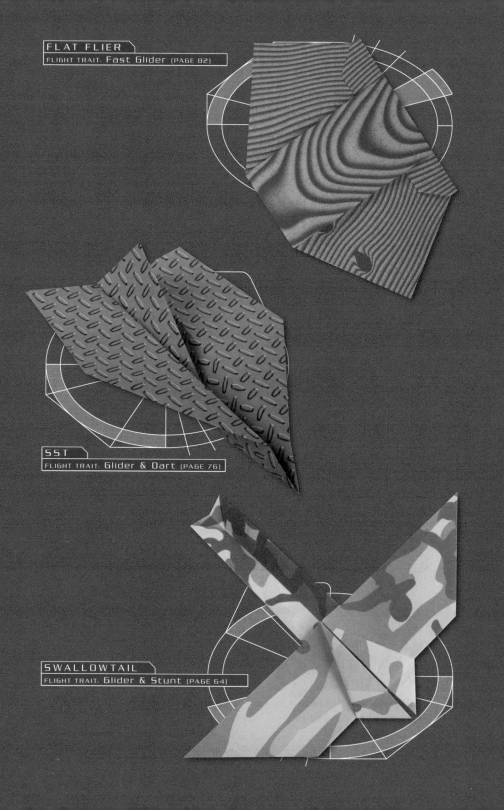

FLAT FLIER
FLIGHT TRAIT: Fast Glider [PAGE 82]

SST
FLIGHT TRAIT: Glider & Dart [PAGE 76]

SWALLOWTAIL
FLIGHT TRAIT: Glider & Stunt [PAGE 64]

GLIDERS

"We sailed a thousand gliders from the Eiffel Tower,
and picked one up several miles away."
—George S. Schairer, The Boeing Company

The main characteristic of a glider is that it stays in the air a long time. That is why glider designs are always the winners in the Time Aloft categories in paper airplane contests around the world. Gliders typically have large wing areas and light bodies. They can soar with the wind and lift higher aided by thermals. Gliders also can perform stunts when thrown hard, or if they are trimmed to loop, roll, or dive. The Happy Flapper, Level Track Delta, and Saber Tooth are reliable fliers that are fun to experiment with in a variety of conditions.

Flying Wing

Basic aeronautics: A large wing surface provides more lift. This clever model has plenty of both. Similar flying wing designs have won Time Aloft titles, including the historic First International Paper Airplane Competition.

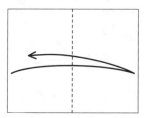

1. White side up, fold in half short edge to short edge, and unfold.

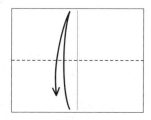

2. Fold in half again, long edge to long edge, and unfold.

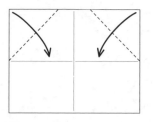

3. Fold down the top corners to the horizontal crease.

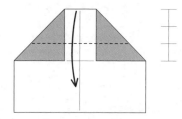

4. Fold down the top edge ⅔ of the distance between the top edge and the horizontal crease.

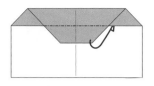

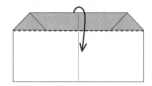

5 Mountain-fold the flap into the pocket underneath.

6 Fold down the flap on the existing horizontal crease.

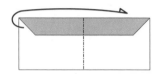

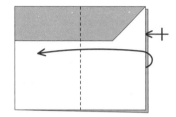

7 Mountain-fold in half along the existing vertical crease.

8 Fold both wings in half.

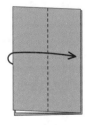

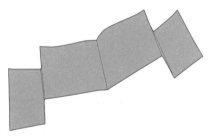

9 Fold the wings back in half, matching both sides.

10 The finished Flying Wing. ■

Flight Plan

Adjust the wings to match the dihedral angle shown above.

Hold the raw-edged end with your fingers on top and your thumb on the bottom. Gently launch forward, releasing the Flying Wing as you extend your arm in one smooth motion. For longer flights, stand on a chair and release.

This model flies best indoors.

MD-20

Its dramatic profile, with swept-back wings and a straight trailing edge, makes this delta-winged plane (named after the Greek letter, Δ) a speedy, stable flier. MD-20 honors former McDonnell Aircraft Corporation's Irl R. Otto, who submitted this traditional design for the historic First International Airplane Competition. It's a superb glider!

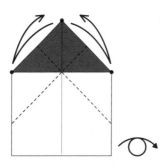

1 Begin with the Airplane Fold (page 16). Fold the top point to the bottom point of the colored triangle in both directions. Turn over.

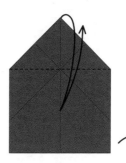

2 Fold down the top point. Crease, and unfold. Turn over.

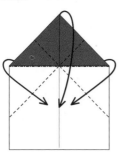

3 Collapse the top point along the existing creases.

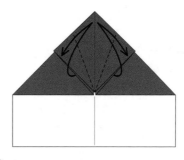

4 Fold the lower sloping edges to the existing center crease. Crease, and unfold.

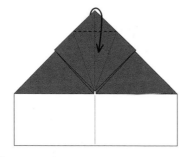

5 Fold down the top point across the end of the creases made in Step **4**.

6 Tuck the corners of the flaps folded in Step **4** into the pockets on the sides of the top triangle.

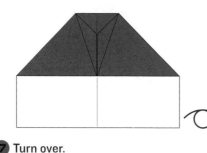

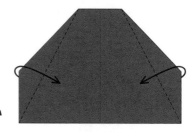

7 Turn over.

8 Fold both winglets along the angles shown.

9 Fold the winglets again, matching the upper sloping edges together.

10 Unfold the winglets so the flaps made in Steps **8** and **9** are at an angle of 90 degrees to each other.

11 The finished MD-20.

Flight Plan

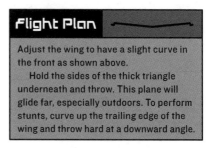

Adjust the wing to have a slight curve in the front as shown above.

Hold the sides of the thick triangle underneath and throw. This plane will glide far, especially outdoors. To perform stunts, curve up the trailing edge of the wing and throw hard at a downward angle.

Swallowtail

A true classic, the Swallowtail is renowned for its gliding abilities, both indoors and out. Its thick nose makes it a sturdy flier. It can also perform stunts, swoop, and dive like a real swallow. With its heavier body offset by a feather-weight tail, the Swallowtail mimics a real bird's body proportions, too! If you choose, you can also fold this plane from origami paper: Form the body from one square and cut about one-third off another square for the tail.

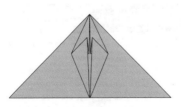

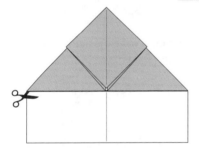

1 Complete Steps **1–3** of the MD-20 (page 62). Cut the tail off the body of the plane. Set aside the tail until Step **4**.

2 Rabbit-ear-fold (page 17) the sloping sides to the center crease, making the "ear" point forward.

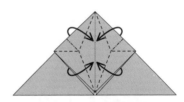

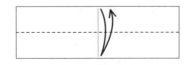

3 Set aside the body until Step **10**.

4 Fold the tail in half, long edge to long edge. Crease, and unfold.

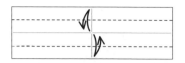

5 Fold the long edges to the center crease. Crease, and unfold.

6 Fold the corners in on the left side to the creases made in Step **5**.

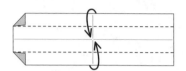

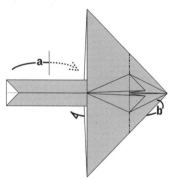

7 Fold the long edges back to the center crease.

8 Airplane-fold (page 16) the corners on the right side to the center.

9 Fold the tail in half and inside-reverse-fold (page 14) the left side. Crease, and unfold.

10 a. Insert the tail into the body as far as it will go.
b. Mountain-fold the body underneath, except for the rabbit-ear flaps. Crease firmly.

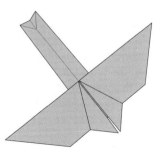

11 The finished Swallowtail. ▄

Flight Plan

Adjust the wings to have a slight curve in the front as shown.

Hold the sides of the thick triangle underneath and throw. Adjust the tail's elevator to perform stunts or to smooth out a glide. This plane is a good outdoor flier. Try throwing the Swallowtail vertically upward as hard as you can!

Time Aloft

Andy Chipling's modified classic glider achieved a Time Aloft World Record of 20.9 seconds, a triumph for Britain. However, in 1998, the record was firmly returned to the USA with a time of 27.6 seconds. Andy is also responsible for writing the rules that Guinness follows for setting paper airplane records.

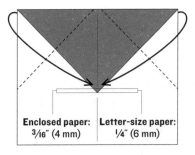

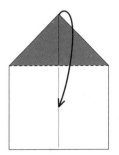

Enclosed paper:	Letter-size paper:
3/16″ (4 mm)	1/4″ (6 mm)

1 Begin with the Airplane Fold (page 16). Fold down the top point along the bottom edges of the flaps.

2 **Softly** fold down the corners to just above the bottom point (see measurements), leaving an even gap at the top edge. Do not crease hard; this will give the wing a rounded, leading-edge-airfoil shape that increases its lift.

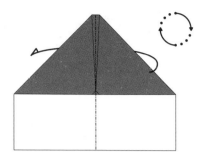

3 Fold up the tiny corner to lock the two flaps.

4 Mountain-fold the plane in half. Rotate ¼-turn clockwise.

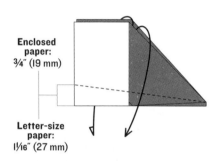

Enclosed paper: 3/4″ (19 mm)

Letter-size paper: 1¹/₁₆″ (27 mm)

5 Fold down the wings on the angle shown. Match the edges carefully.

6 The finished Time Aloft. ▓

Flight Plan

Adjust the wings to have a flat T-shape, as shown above, while holding the plane.

Throw the Time Aloft hard and high into the air. This will enable it to soar very far after stabilizing. When outside, you'll be chasing it—if you throw it from a window or a rooftop, just say good-bye!

Make a second Time Aloft plane for performing stunts, since the wings are very sensitive to any curling of the paper. Adjust the elevons for loops and rolls.

Daisy's Flier

A sturdy and reliable flier—throw it hard—Daisy's Flier is a **Nick Robinson** design, named for his daughter. Nick's unique folding sequence is more elegant than the traditional methods, which use an origami waterbomb base in the first steps, and creates a neater nose. It is also used in the **MD-20, Swallowtail,** and **Waterbomber (pages 62, 64, 100).**

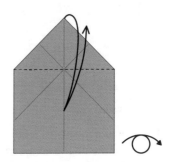

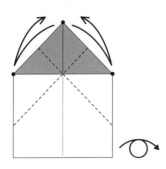

1 Begin with the Airplane Fold (page 16). Fold the top point to the bottom point of the colored triangle in both directions. Turn over.

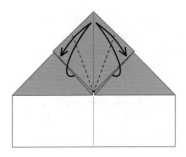

2 Fold down the top point. Crease, and unfold. Turn over.

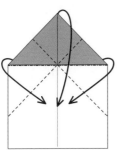

3 Collapse the top point along the existing creases.

4 Fold the lower sloping edges to the existing center crease. Crease, and unfold.

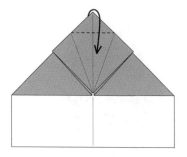

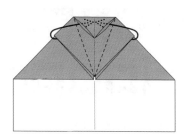

5 Fold down the top point across the end of the creases made in Step **4**.

6 Tuck the corners of the flaps folded in Step 4 into the pockets on the sides of the top triangle.

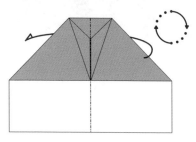

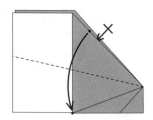

7 Mountain-fold the plane in half. Rotate ¼-turn clockwise.

8 Starting at the right, fold the wing so that its leading edge touches the point shown. Repeat with the other wing, matching the edges carefully.

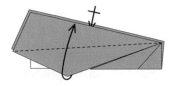

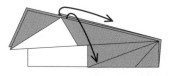

9 Fold up the winglet, matching the leading edge with the fold made in Step **8**. Repeat on the other side.

10 Unfold the wings and winglets to match the Flight Plan below.

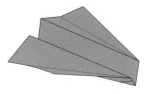

Flight Plan

Adjust the wings shown above; adjust the winglets to have the slightest angle.

Hold the middle of the fuselage and throw. Try different throwing speeds and angles for fun flights. Daisy's Flier is great indoors or out.

11 The finished Daisy's Flier. ▨

Happy Flapper

Aloft on a breeze, the Happy Flapper's wings may appear to flap in the wind! A distance flier, this design by Stephen Weiss incorporates his trademark wing creases and trim— simple to fold and easy to fly.

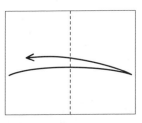

1 White side up, fold in half short edge to short edge, and unfold.

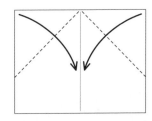

2 Airplane-fold (page 16) the corners to the center crease.

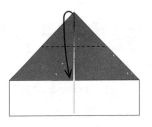

3 Fold down the top corner to the horizontal edges.

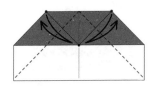

4 Airplane-fold the top edge of both sides to the center crease. Crease, and unfold.

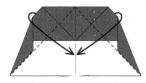

5 Fold the raw vertical edges on the outer sides to the creases made in Step **4**.

6 Refold the sides in on the existing creases made in Step **4**.

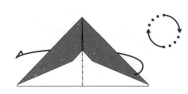

7 Mountain-fold the plane in half. Rotate ¼-turn clockwise.

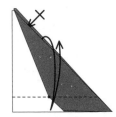

8 Fold down the wing parallel to the fuselage and through the point shown. Crease, and unfold. Repeat with the other wing.

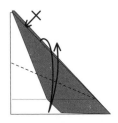

9 Fold down the wing so the leading edge lines up with the crease made in Step **8**. Crease, and unfold. Repeat with the other wing.

10 Fold the winglet's tip down to the crease made in Step **9**. Crease, and unfold. Repeat with the other winglet.

11 The finished Happy Flapper. Follow the Flight Plan to adjust the wings and winglets. ■

Flight Plan

Adjust the wings and winglets to match the dihedral angle shown above.

Throw with a gentle to moderate speed, depending on whether you're indoors or out. The Happy Flapper is a reliable glider that can be carried away by the wind!

Tube Glider

The Tube Glider will glide gracefully from any height, whether you launch it from the top of a bunk bed or off a tower. First published in the 1970s, this gliding toy is beautiful in the simplicity of its design. Nobody seems to know how old it is, or who invented it.

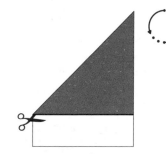

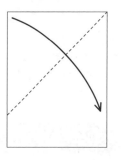

1 Fold down the top edge to line up with the right edge.

2 Cut the lower portion off, leaving the folded triangle behind. This is how to make a square from any rectangle. Rotate ⅜-turn counterclockwise.

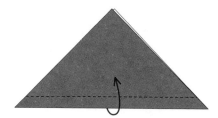

3 Fold over a small strip, keeping the crease parallel to the folded edge.

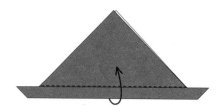

4 Fold over the strip again, keeping the crease parallel to the folded edge.

5 Curl the triangle into a tube and insert one tab into the other. It may help to rub the folded edge over the corner of a table for a smooth curve.

6 The finished Tube Glider. ▪

Flight Plan ⬤

Adjust the Tube Glider to be as evenly round as possible, smoothing out any folded bumps.

Hold the tail end as shown. Gently launch forward, releasing the Tube Glider as you extend your arm in one smooth motion. For longer flights, stand on a chair and release, or launch from a window. It may glide out of sight!

Wind Hawk

A glider that can even hover in the wind, Stephen Weiss' Wind Hawk features a stable fuselage. Take it outdoors and watch it waft on a thermal.

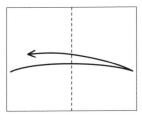

1 White side up, fold in half short edge to short edge, and unfold.

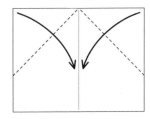

2 Airplane-fold (page 16) the corners to the center crease.

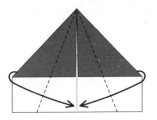

3 Airplane-fold the sides to the center crease.

4 Fold down the top point to the point indicated.

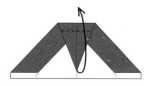

5 While holding down the top pointed flap and keeping it centered, swivel the sides out to the position shown. Note that in Step **6**, the inner folded edge intersects the existing crease.

6 Fold up the top pointed flap as far as it will go.

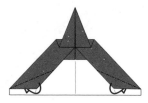

7 Mountain-fold the bottom edge of each flap under as far as it will go.

8 Mountain-fold the plane in half. Rotate ¼-turn clockwise.

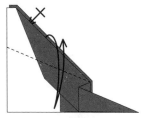
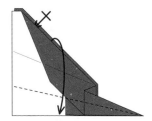

9 Fold down the wing flap on the existing crease, and unfold. Repeat with the other wing flap.

10 Fold down the wing, bisecting the nose on the angle shown. Repeat with the other wing.

11 The finished Wind Hawk. ■

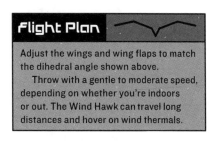

Flight Plan

Adjust the wings and wing flaps to match the dihedral angle shown above.

Throw with a gentle to moderate speed, depending on whether you're indoors or out. The Wind Hawk can travel long distances and hover on wind thermals.

SST

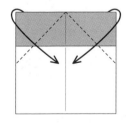

This plane won't break the sound barrier, but the SST is designed to be a speedy flier. To give the SST more stability, this sleek and modern design by Stephen Weiss incorporates an Inside Reverse Fold for a tail fin, as well as additional control surfaces to trim.

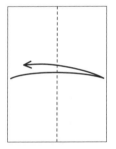

1 White side up, fold in half long edge to long edge, and unfold.

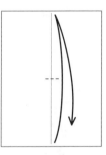

2 Bring short edge to short edge just to mark the center with a small pinch, and unfold.

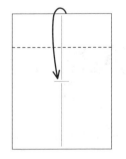

3 Fold down the upper edge to the pinch mark made in Step **2**.

4 Airplane-fold (page 16) the top corners to the center crease.

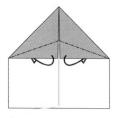
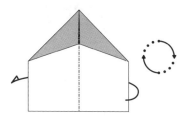

5 Mountain-fold the bottom flaps, tucking them underneath the edge of the layer below.

6 Mountain-fold the plane in half. Rotate ¼-turn clockwise.

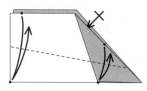
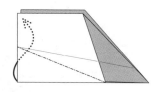

7 Fold down the wing so its edges line up with the points shown on the fuselage. Crease, and unfold. Repeat with the other wing.

8 Inside-reverse-fold (page 14) the tail fin up, in between the fuselage and wings.

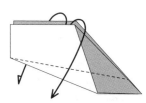

9 Fold down the wings on the existing creases made in Step **7**.

10 The finished SST. ■

Flight Plan ———◇———

Adjust the wings to match the dihedral angle shown above.

Throw with a gentle to moderate speed, depending on whether you're indoors or out. If the SST tends to fly downward, adjust the elevons slightly upward. Correct turns by adjusting the tail fin.

Hang Glider

This glider carves a graceful arc through the air. Designed by famed paperfolder Kunihiko Kasahara, who "stubbornly prefers to use square paper," this glider is ideal for indoor flights.

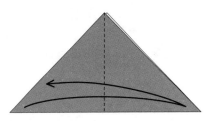

1 Begin with a square folded in half as shown. Fold in half again. Crease, and unfold.

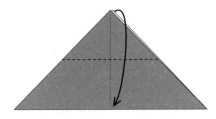

2 Fold the triangle in half so the top points align with the center crease.

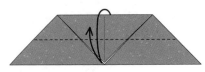

3 Fold in half again. Crease, and unfold.

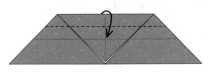

4 Fold down the top to the crease made in Step **3**.

5 Turn over.

6 Fold in half, aligning the left and right bottom points. The thick layers at the top edge will fall out of alignment but do not realign. Crease firmly.

7 Fold down the wing so the leading edge lines up with the center edge. Crease, and unfold. Repeat with the other wing.

8 Fold down the wing again so the crease made in Step 7 lines up with the center edge. Crease, and unfold. Repeat with the other wing.

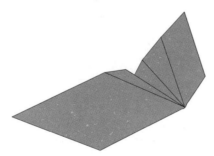

9 The finished Hang Glider. Follow the Flight Plan to adjust the wings. ▪

Flight Plan

Adjust the wings to match the dihedral angle shown above.

Hold the tail end with your index finger inside the fuselage and your thumb and middle finger gripping the bottom. Gently launch forward, releasing the Hang Glider as you extend your arm in one smooth motion. For longer flights, stand on a chair and release.

This model flies best indoors.

Little Bird

A model of simplicity and beauty, **Little Bird** is such an efficient flier that it even glides upside down. Created by **Makoto Yamaguchi**, it is a terrific plane for kids to fold and fly.

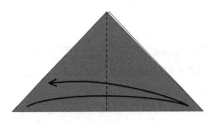

1 Begin with a square folded in half as shown. Fold in half again. Crease, and unfold.

2 Fold up the bottom edge at about ⅓ of the height of the triangle.

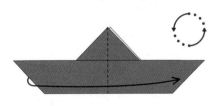

3 Fold in half. Rotate ¼-turn counterclockwise.

4 Fold down the wing on the angle shown. Repeat with the other wing.

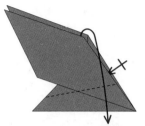

5 Fold down the wing again on the angle shown. Repeat with the other wing.

6 Follow the Flight Plan and refer to the photo to adjust the wings.

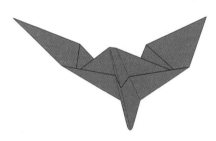

7 The finished Little Bird. ▪

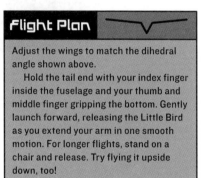

Flight Plan

Adjust the wings to match the dihedral angle shown above.

Hold the tail end with your index finger inside the fuselage and your thumb and middle finger gripping the bottom. Gently launch forward, releasing the Little Bird as you extend your arm in one smooth motion. For longer flights, stand on a chair and release. Try flying it upside down, too!

This model flies best indoors.

Flat Flier

Paul Jackson's abstract, super-cool Flat Flier will fly a long way at high speed, but it's tricky to throw, as are most flat planes. Follow the Flight Plan to master the launch technique.

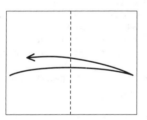

1. White side up, fold in half short edge to short edge, and unfold.

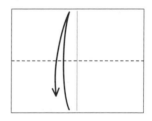

2. Fold in half again, long edge to long edge, and unfold.

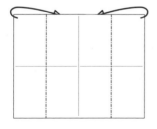

3. Mountain-fold the side edges to the vertical crease.

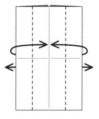

4. Flip-Out Fold: Fold the side edges to the center, and allow the flaps from the rear to flip to the front.

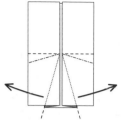

5 Swivel out the lower corners, folding on the X-ray View line. Pleat the Mountain Fold above the existing horizontal crease.

6 Fold the upper section in half, tucking the corners under the flaps made in Step **5**.

7 Fold the upper section in half again, tucking the corners under the flaps made in Step **5**.

8 Turn over.

9 Mountain-fold the corners under to lock.

10 The finished Flat Flier. ■

Flight Plan

There isn't a dihedral angle for this plane.

Hold the tail end with your index finger inside the fuselage and your thumb and middle finger gripping the bottom. Launch by bending your elbow and "flicking it firmly forward." Don't throw it high into the air.

This model flies best indoors or outside on a calm day.

Butterfly

This exquisite design flies like a glider and will even flutter if made from smaller, thinner paper. According to its designer, Paul Jackson, the key to successful execution of this plane is to take your time with Step 2.

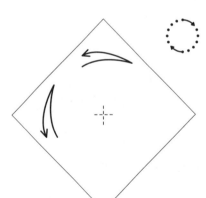

1. Begin with a square, white side up. Fold along both diagonals marking the center with a small pinch mark. Unfold back to a square, white side up. Rotate ⅛-turn clockwise.

2. Fold up the bottom half through the center creases. Line up the edges so that **AB** is twice as long as **CD**. Use the X-ray View line as a guide, but then measure and adjust for perfect symmetry.

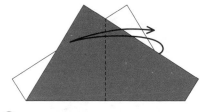

3 Fold in half. Crease, and unfold.

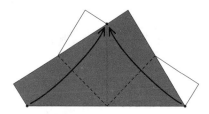

4 Airplane-fold (page 16) the bottom corners up to the center crease.

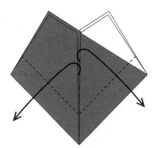

5 Fold down the wings. Look at Step **6** to see the shape you are trying to match.

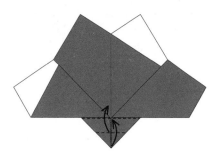

6 Fold the bottom point to the horizontal edge, then fold again, level with the edge.

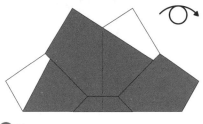

7 Turn over.

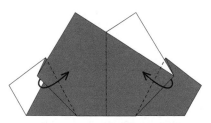

8 Fold the top flaps inward. Make a shallow Mountain Fold on the center crease.

9 The finished Butterfly. ■

Flight Plan

Adjust the wings to match the dihedral angle shown above.

Hold the tail end with your index finger inside the fuselage and your thumb and middle finger gripping the bottom. Gently launch forward, releasing the Butterfly as you extend your arm in one smooth motion. For longer flights, stand on a chair and release.

This model flies best indoors.

Saber Tooth

A robust flier that responds well to a hard throw, it can even fly upside down! This classic design has been rediscovered and renamed by brain researcher **Chou Hung**.

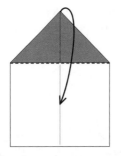

1 Begin with the Airplane Fold (page 16). Fold down the top point along the bottom edges of the flaps.

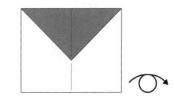

2 Turn over.

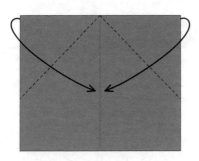

3 Airplane-fold the side edges to the horizontal crease.

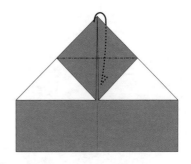

4 Mountain-fold the top point in half toward the back.

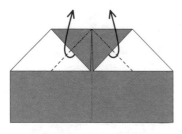

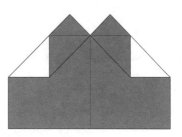

5 Squash-fold (page 16) the "teeth" by lifting the flap and aligning the side edges with the top edge.

6 Fold the upper section in half, tucking the corners under the flaps made in Step **5**.

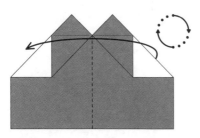

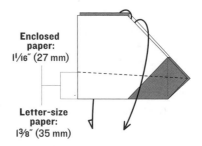

Enclosed paper: 1¹/₁₆" (27 mm)

Letter-size paper: 1³/₈" (35 mm)

7 Valley-fold the plane in half. Rotate ¼-turn clockwise.

8 Fold down the wings on the angle shown. Match the edges carefully.

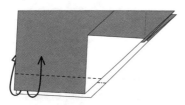

9 Fold the winglets at a right angle to the wings. Open the wings.

10 The finished Saber Tooth. ◼

Flight Plan

Adjust the wings to match the dihedral angle shown above.

This plane is perfect for hard throws outdoors, on windy or calm days. For long-duration flights, throw upward, slightly tilting left or right. Trim if necessary, though the angle folded in Step **8** helps minimize the need to adjust this plane. Try launching upside down.

Level Track Delta

A superb glider, the Level Track Delta has unusual winglets that channel air beneath the plane, making it very stable in flight. Stephen Weiss named this plane for its ability to fly straight and level to the ground. This model will fly outdoors, but may require additional trim if it's windy.

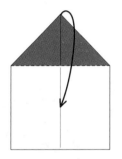

1 Begin with the Airplane Fold (page 16). Fold down the top point along the bottom edges of the flaps.

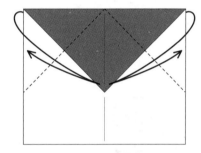

2 Airplane-fold the side edges to the vertical crease. Crease, and unfold.

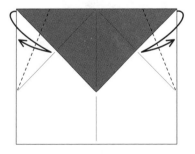

3 Fold the side edges to the creases made in Step **2**. Crease, and unfold.

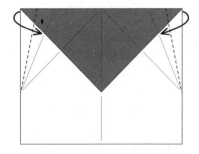

4 Fold the side edges to the creases made in Step **3**.

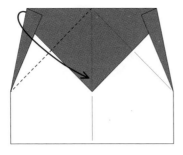

5 Fold the left side to the center crease on the existing crease.

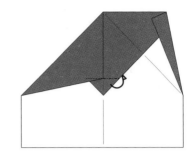

6 Mountain-fold the small triangle underneath at the point shown.

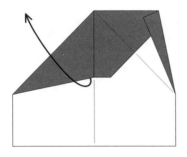

7 Unfold the left flap as shown in Step **5**.

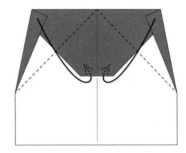

8 Airplane-fold the sides in, and tuck the raw-edge flaps underneath the fold made in Step **6**.

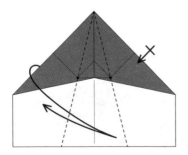

9 Fold the wing on the angle shown. Note the fold line intersects with the hidden triangle underneath. Repeat with the other wing.

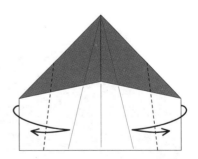

10 Fold the raw side edges of the wings to align with the creases made in Step **9**. Crease, and unfold.

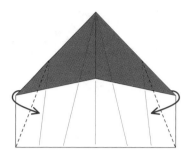

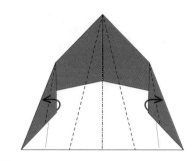

11 Fold the winglets on the angle shown.

12 Fold the edges of the winglets to the folded edge. Refer to the Flight Plan to form the final shape using the existing creases.

13 The finished Level Track Delta. ■

Flight Plan

Adjust the wings and winglets to the rear profile shown above.

Throw with a moderate speed, whether you're indoors or out. The Level Track Delta should glide far and land safely on the ground. If it takes a nose dive, trim the elevons up just a bit to achieve a level flight. Make sure the winglets underneath are at 90-degree angles and the dihedral angle is flat when the wings are at rest.

Manta Ray

Born in Laos, Thay Yang grew up with the roar of fighter jets streaking across the sky. Most of his designs are based on actual military aircraft from several nations. Yang's fantasy airplane design, the Manta Ray, is a fairly finicky glider. Flying this model requires precise folding and careful trim.

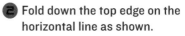

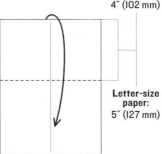

Enclosed paper:
4″ (102 mm)

Letter-size paper:
5″ (127 mm)

1. White side up, fold in half long edge to long edge, and unfold.

2. Fold down the top edge on the horizontal line as shown.

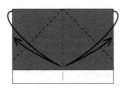

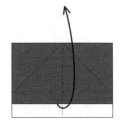

3. Airplane-fold (page 16) the side edges to the horizontal crease. Crease, and unfold.

4. Unfold.

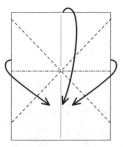

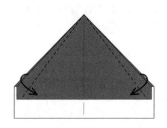

5 Collapse the top edge along the existing creases.

6 Fold the top flap's sloping edges toward the center on the angle shown.

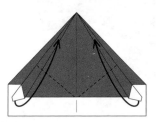

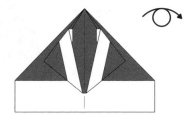

7 Fold up the top flaps so their sloping edges align with each other. Leave a small gap in the middle.

8 Turn over.

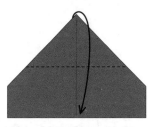

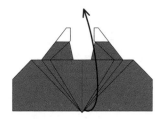

9 Fold down the top layer as far as it will go.

10 Unfold.

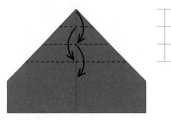

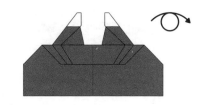

11 Fold down the top layer in thirds between the top point and the existing crease made in Step **9**.

12 Turn over.

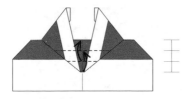

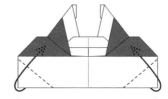

13 Fold up the top layer in thirds to the horizontal edge.

14 Fold up the bottom corners on the angle shown, tucking the points underneath the flap.

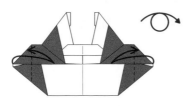

15 Fold the winglets toward the center. Crease, and unfold. Turn over and adjust the dihedral angle and winglets as shown in the Flight Plan.

16 The finished Manta Ray. ■

Flight Plan

Adjust the wings and winglets to the profile shown above.

Hold the tail end with your index finger inside the fuselage and your thumb and middle finger gripping the bottom. Gently launch forward, releasing the Manta Ray as you extend your arm in one smooth motion. For longer flights, stand on a chair and release.

This model flies best indoors.

Strider

The Strider is an excellent glider, reliably producing fast and straight flights. The fuselage angle is key to giving the plane its lift without any additional trim. The designer, Sipho Mabona, has been a paper airplane enthusiast since childhood.

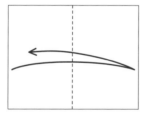

1 White side up, fold in half short edge to short edge, and unfold.

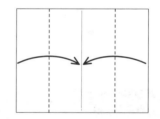

2 Fold the side edges to the center crease.

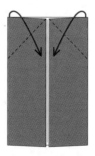

3 Airplane-fold (page 16) the corners to the center crease.

4 Mountain-fold the top corner back along the horizontal edges. Turn over.

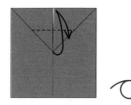

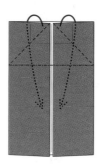

5 Fold the bottom point to the top edge. Crease, and unfold. Unfold the paper to Step **3**, and turn over.

6 Swivel down the corners under the side flaps using the existing creases. The top edges of the paper will align with the center crease.

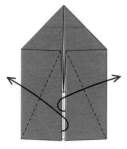

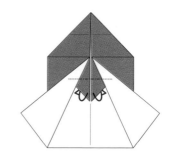

7 Fold the top flaps outward on the angle shown.

8 Mountain-fold the tips underneath along the existing creases.

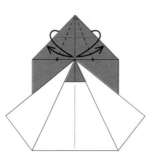

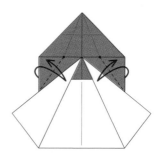

9 Fold the upper sloping edges to the center crease, but only to the horizontal folded edges. Crease, and unfold.

10 Fold the side edges on the angle shown, but only to the horizontal folded edges, meeting the creases made in Step **9**. Crease, and unfold.

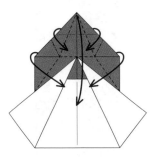

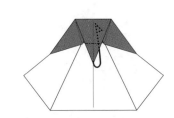

11 Collapse the top triangle along the existing Valley Fold creases. Mountain Folds will form when you flatten the point.

12 Mountain-fold the tip behind the layers underneath to lock the nose together.

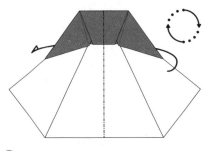

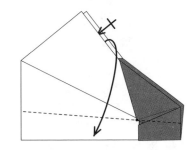

13 Mountain-fold the plane in half. Rotate ¼-turn clockwise.

14 Fold the wing down, bisecting the nose on the angle shown, making sure the crease goes through the point marked. Repeat with the other wing.

15 The finished Strider. ▪

Flight Plan

Adjust the wings to match the dihedral angle shown above.

The Strider's performance and lift depend greatly on the fuselage angle folded in Step 14. Practice with slightly different angles to get just the right glide without additional trim. Throw at moderate speed, varying the angle if desired. This plane flies very well indoors or out!

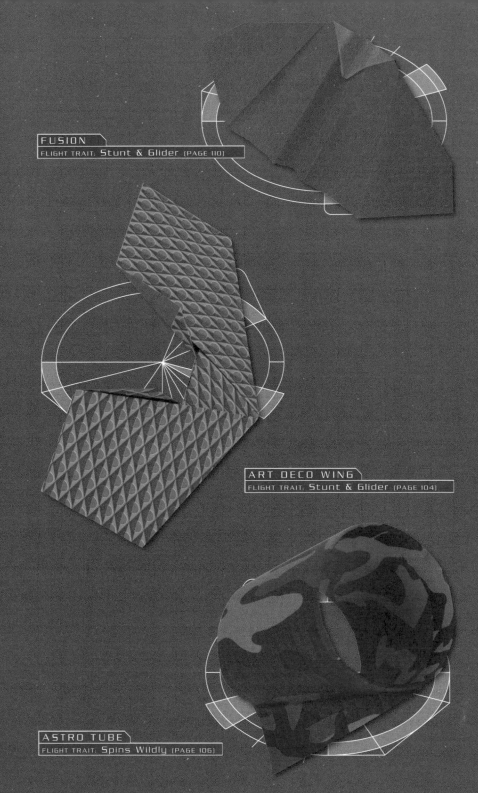

FUSION
FLIGHT TRAIT: Stunt & Glider [PAGE 110]

ART DECO WING
FLIGHT TRAIT: Stunt & Glider [PAGE 104]

ASTRO TUBE
FLIGHT TRAIT: Spins Wildly [PAGE 106]

STUNTS

"**Stunt paper planes can be thrown at practically any angle,
and at various speeds; you just need to experiment.**"
—Sara Gray, **Easy Paper Airplanes**

Stunt planes do tricks—instead of flying long and straight, they can
"bend" a traditional flight into a loop-the-loop or a crazy spin; they
can even do a "round trip," returning right to your hands! By simply
bending the wing and rudder surfaces a teensy bit, you can control
a stunt plane's flight to amaze onlookers and friends. The Crazy
Stunter is folded to fly silly; however, the Fusion and Immortal are
serious stunt planes designed with more predictable flight in mind.
Stunts may need careful trim and some "trial-and-error-and-error-
and-error" depending on how hard or at what angle you launch them.

Waterbomber

Based on the same basic folds used in the **MD-20** (page 62), this pumped up plane adds some special features: radical winglets, "engine" nacelles, and pronounced elevons to encourage loops and wild flights. A sturdy flat nose allows it to withstand crashes without crumpling. Its name comes from the water-bomb base beginning many origami models.

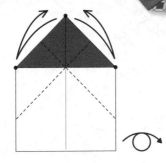

1 Begin with the Airplane Fold (page 16). Fold the top point to the bottom point of the colored triangle in both directions. Turn over.

2 Fold down the top point. Crease, and unfold. Turn over.

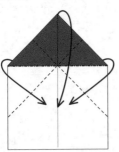

3 Collapse the top point along the existing creases.

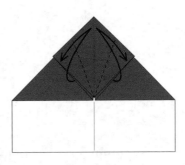

4 Fold the lower sloping edges to the existing center crease. Crease, and unfold.

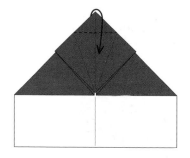

5 Fold down the top point across the end of the creases made in Step **4**.

6 Tuck the corners of the flaps folded in Step **4** into the pockets on the sides of the top triangle.

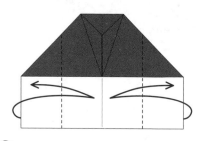

7 Fold the sides to the center crease. Crease, and unfold.

8 Mountain-fold both winglets under to the creases made in Step **7**.

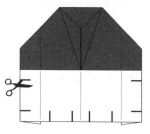

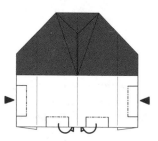

9 Cut slits for nacelles and elevons.

10 Inside-reverse-fold (page 14) the nacelles and mountain-fold the elevons slightly. Refold the winglets to match the Flight Plan below.

11 The finished Waterbomber. ■

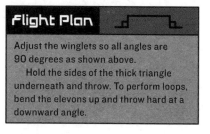

Flight Plan

Adjust the winglets so all angles are 90 degrees as shown above.

Hold the sides of the thick triangle underneath and throw. To perform loops, bend the elevons up and throw hard at a downward angle.

Pointy Bird

Generous wing and rudder surface areas, along with front winglets (called canards), make Pointy Bird adjustable for stunt flying—and keep it from stalling in the air. Nick Robinson designed this spunky little plane to perform well indoors and out.

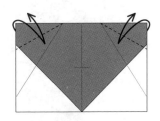

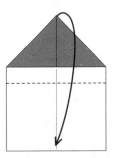

1 Begin with the Airplane Fold (page 16). Fold down the top point to the bottom edge.

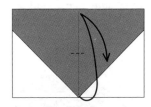

2 Bring up the bottom point to the top edge just to mark the center with a small pinch, and unfold.

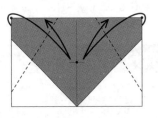

3 Airplane-fold the upper corners' edges to the pinch mark. Crease, and unfold.

4 Fold down the top edges to the creaselines made in Step 3. Crease, and unfold.

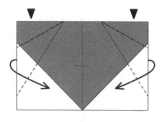

5 Swivel in the lower layer on the existing creases made in Step **3** while making Mountain Folds on the top layer's existing creases.

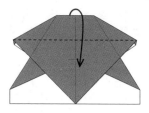

6 Fold down the top section along the widest points as shown.

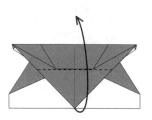

7 Fold up the bottom corner along the horizontal edge as shown.

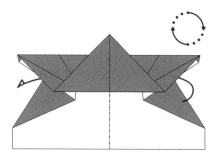

8 Mountain-fold the plane in half. Rotate ¼-turn clockwise.

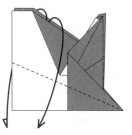

9 Fold down the wings to match the Flight Plan below.

10 The finished Pointy Bird. ■

Flight Plan

Adjust the wings to match the dihedral angle shown above.

This plane is perfect for hard throws outdoors on windy or calm days. Trim the elevons for stunts. You can also trim slightly to get a straight, long glide, too. Its heavy nose and large wing surface give it good stability for gliding.

Art Deco Wing

Michael LaFosse named his beautiful Art Deco Wing because of its clean lines and simple shapes. It acts as a glider or a stunt plane depending on what angle and how hard you throw it. The Art Deco Wing is great for launching from atop a building or hill.

1 Begin with a square folded in half as shown. Fold up the bottom corners to the top corner.

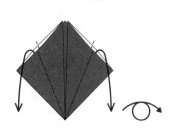

2 Squash-fold (page 16) the upper flaps down, flattening the center folded edge on the creases made in Step **1** to make a kite shape. Turn over.

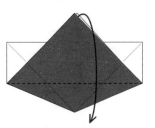

3 Fold down the top layer along its widest point.

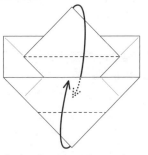

4 Tuck the the top point underneath and fold the bottom point to the fold made in Step **3**.

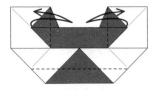

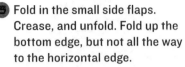

5 Fold in the small side flaps. Crease, and unfold. Fold up the bottom edge, but not all the way to the horizontal edge.

6 Fold the bottom side corners so the raw sloping edges align with the horizontal folded edge.

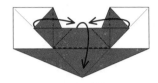

7 Fold the entire front flap around and tuck it underneath itself.

8 Pull down the central flap bringing in the two side flaps on the existing creases made in Step **5**. Squash the new creases flat.

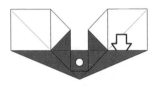

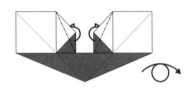

9 Hide the flap made in Step **8** underneath the nose layer.

10 Mountain-fold the winglets along the folded edge underneath. Turn over.

11 The finished Art Deco Wing. Follow the Flight Plan to adjust the winglets. ■

Flight Plan

Adjust the winglets to match the angle shown above.

Throw with your index finger on top and your thumb on the bottom of the back of its nose. Launch into the wind for fluttering flights; or throw upward as hard and high as you can for long, smooth glides when it's calm outdoors. Make loops by throwing hard downward and trimming the elevons up a little.

Astro Tube

This unusual-looking model spins wildly through the air when it is flung like a football. Customize the Astro Tube before flight, though: the fin can be angled either way, depending on how you join the ends together in Step 4, to accommodate left- or right-handed throwing. Stephen Weiss adapted a similar tube by the late Akira Yoshizawa to create this unique flier.

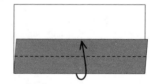

1. White side up, fold up the bottom edge at about 1/3 of the height of the rectangle.

2. Fold up the bottom edge to the raw edge.

3. Fold up the bottom edge to the new folded edge. Crease, and unfold.

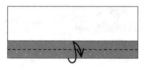

Enclosed paper:
1⅛″ (29 mm)

Letter-size paper:
1½″ (38 mm)

4. Curl the rectangle into a tube and insert one edge into the other. It may help to rub the folded edge over the corner of a table for a smooth curve. **Note:** Insert the right end into the left end for a right-handed Tube; reverse for a left-handed Tube.

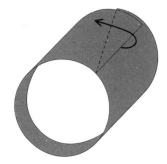

5 Hold at the seam and fold in the leading edge on the existing creases made in Step **3**.

6 Fold the fin up from the upper overlapped layer so it's perpendicular to the Tube on the angle shown.

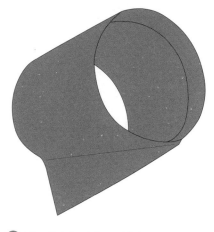

7 The finished Astro Tube. ▪

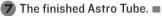

Flight Plan

Adjust the wing to be perpendicular to the tube as shown above.

Hold the Astro Tube near the rim between the thumb and fingers with the fin on the bottom. Throw the Tube underhanded, letting it spin off your fingers. It will spin through the air. You can also throw it overhanded, as if you were throwing a football. The Astro Tube works best indoors, but it's fun to watch its crazy flight paths in the breezes outdoors, too!

Crazy Stunter

Opposing winglets plus an additional winglet underneath are features that make this plane's name especially appropriate: Crazy Stunter goes for wild and unpredictable rides. Fly Andy Chipling's adaptation of a simple stunt plane outdoors— in any weather but rain!

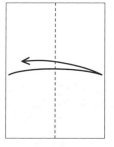

1 White side up, fold in half long edge to long edge, and unfold.

2 Fold down the upper-left corner so the top raw edge aligns with the right raw edge.

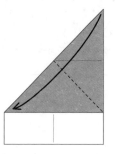

3 Fold down the top point so the folded edges align with each other.

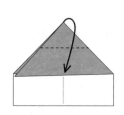

4 Fold down the top corner to meet the horizontal edge.

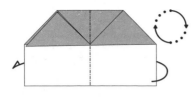

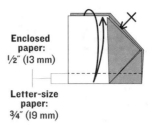

Enclosed
paper:
½″ (13 mm)

Letter-size
paper:
¾″ (19 mm)

5 Mountain-fold the plane in half. Rotate ¼-turn clockwise.

6 Fold down the wing parallel to the fuselage as shown. Crease, and unfold. Repeat with the other wing.

7 Fold down the upper flap's point to meet the crease made in Step **6**. Crease, and unfold.

8 Fold down the upper flap's point to meet the point across from the bottom of the lower sloping edge.

Enclosed
paper:
½″ (13 mm)

Letter-size
paper:
¾″ (19 mm)

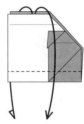

9 Valley-fold down both winglets together. Crease, and unfold.

10 Bring down both wings on the existing creases and follow the Flight Plan to set the winglets.

11 The finished Crazy Stunter. ▪

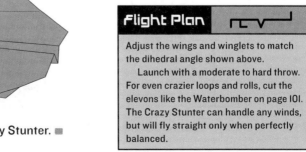

Flight Plan

Adjust the wings and winglets to match the dihedral angle shown above.

Launch with a moderate to hard throw. For even crazier loops and rolls, cut the elevons like the Waterbomber on page 101. The Crazy Stunter can handle any winds, but will fly straight only when perfectly balanced.

Fusion

Easy to fold and fly, the Fusion has a beautiful wing structure that keeps it floating high for stunts or gliding. After several crash-lands its initial springiness loosens up and the wings begin to flap in the breeze. The Fusion is one of Darren Thorne's most popular planes among a fleet called Aerogami.

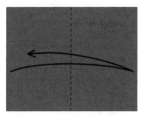

1 Colored side up, fold in half short edge to short edge, and unfold.

2 Fold the side edges to the horizontal crease.

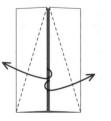

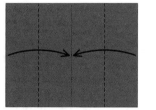

3 Fold the top layers outward at the angle shown.

4 Mountain-fold the bottom edge to the top edge.

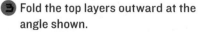

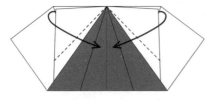

5 Airplane-fold (page 16) the top-layer flaps to the center crease.

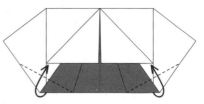

6 Fold the bottom corners so the right sloping edges align with the horizontal edges of the flaps folded in Step **5**.

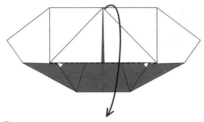

7 Fold down the top triangle at its bottom edge.

8 Mountain-fold the bottom point to the back.

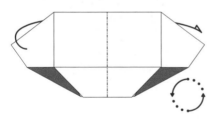

9 Mountain-fold the plane in half. Rotate ¼-turn counterclockwise.

10 Fold down the wings parallel to the fuselage as shown. Match the edges carefully.

11 The finished Fusion. ■

Flight Plan

Adjust the wings to match the dihedral angle shown above.

Throw as hard as you can! The Fusion is a strong flier that can take lots of crash landings, and even "loosens up" the more you fly it. Adjust the elevons for loops, rolls, and fun flights, but don't flatten the wings!

Immortal

Folding this model may be a bit more challenging than others, but the reward for finishing is a plane that has superior flight characteristics for stunts or long-range gliding. Complex wing folds compress a lot of weight in the nose, which makes Immortal a sturdy, acrobatic flier. Sipho Mabona designed this amazing plane while folding a menu in a Chinese restaurant, but it works best folded from regular letter-size paper.

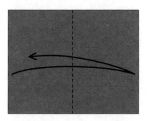

1 Colored side up, fold in half short edge to short edge, and unfold.

2 Mountain-fold the side edges to the center crease.

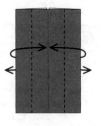

3 Flip-Out Fold: Fold the side edges to the center, and allow the flaps from the rear to flip to the front.

4 Mountain-fold the top half behind the bottom half.

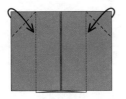

5 Airplane-fold (page 16) the upper corners to the hidden fold lines beneath.

6 Fold up the top layer along the bottom edges of the corners folded in Step **5**.

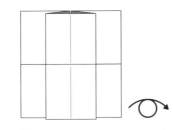

7 Turn over.

8 Fold the upper corners so the side edges align with the upper sloping edges of the top layer.

9 Airplane-fold the upper sloping edges of the top layers to the center crease; do not fold the bottom layers.

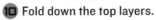
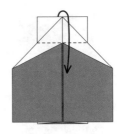

10 Fold down the top layers.

11 Mountain-fold the flap underneath, tucking the corners under the flaps folded in Step **9**.

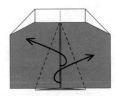

12 Fold out the top-layer flaps on the angles shown.

13 Swivel out the lower corners as far as they will go. Squash the new creases indicated by the Mountain and Valley Fold lines.

14 Mountain-fold the end flaps to the back along the folded edge underneath. Turn over.

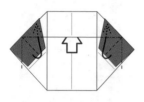

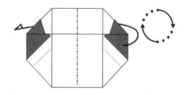

15 Swivel and tuck the flaps folded in Step **14** underneath the top layer as far as they will go.

16 Mountain-fold the plane in half. Rotate ¼-turn clockwise.

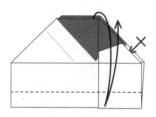

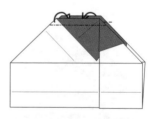

17 Fold down the wing parallel to the fuselage as shown. Crease, and unfold. Repeat with the other wing.

18 Fold the winglets parallel to the fuselage. Shape the wings and winglets according to the Flight Plan below.

19 The finished Immortal. ■

Flight Plan

Adjust the wings and winglets to match the dihedral angle shown above.

The Immortal displays its full performance potential when flown outdoors. Throw as hard as you can upward and expect to chase the plane a long way! Gently raise the elevons to give it more lift and to make it loop or roll.

Housefly

This groundbreaking plane introduced the locked-fuselage design, a feature that enhances durability and aerodynamic performance. Michael LaFosse's simple plane also has winglet-like front surfaces called canards that enhance its stability. Its blunt nose can withstand the rigors of many enjoyable flights (and crashes), and it performs well indoors and out.

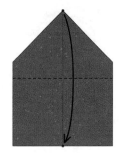

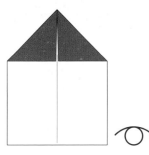

1 Begin with the Airplane Fold (page 16). Turn over.

2 Fold fown the top point to the bottom edge.

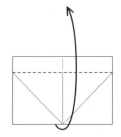

3 Turn over.

4 Fold up the top layer along the hidden raw edges underneath.

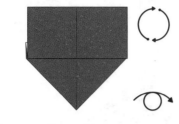

5 Turn over. Rotate ½-turn.

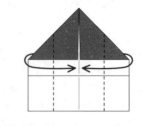

6 Fold the side edges to the center crease.

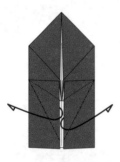

7 Swivel out the top-layer flap of each wing as far as it will go. Squash-fold (page 16) the resulting creases.

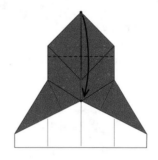

8 Fold down the top point to the point where the top layers meet at the center crease.

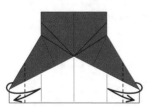

9 Fold in the winglets so the raw edge aligns with the existing crease. Crease, and unfold.

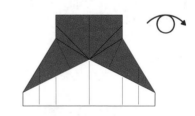

10 Turn over.

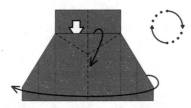

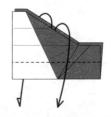

11 Create the fuselage lock by lifting up the small pocket as far as it will go while folding the plane in half. Rotate ¼-turn clockwise.

12 Fold down both wings, matching the top horizontal edge with the bottom of the fuselage. Follow the Flight Plan below to adjust the wings and winglets.

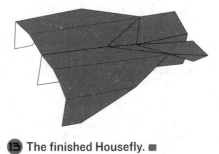

13 The finished Housefly. ■

Flight Plan

Adjust the wings to have only a slight crease and so the winglets are parallel to the fuselage.

This Housefly is perfect for moderate to hard throws outdoors on windy or calm days. For long-duration flights, throw upward. Trim the elevons for added lift or stunts. A locked-fuselage design enables the Housefly to be a very reliable and durable flier, and if it hits the wall, the nose isn't easily damaged.

CRUISE MISSILE
FLIGHT TRAIT: Speedy Dart [PAGE 43]

SABER TOOTH
FLIGHT TRAIT: Glider & Stunt [PAGE 86]

POINTY BIRD
FLIGHT TRAIT: Stunt [PAGE 102]

Where Can I Learn More?

For more information about the contributors to this book, see the following information. The paper airplane designs they've provided are just a tiny sampling of their extraordinary talent. Some of their Web sites contain general tips, galleries of their work, and instructions for additional paper airplane designs you can download.

Several of the creators have published books with many more of their models. Some titles may be out of print, however a search on the Web will likely turn up used copies.

Andy Chipling

The Paper Aircraft Association was founded by Chipling after his long interest in all kinds of aviation. He is also the definitive authority and author of Guinness' World Record Rules for paper airplane contests. Chipling's Web site contains a wide variety of trivia and announcements for paper airplane enthusiasts. He lives in England.
www.paperaircraft.com

Marvin Goody

The qualities Goody aims for in his models include simplicity, elegance, three-dimensionality, and easy landmarks. The folders whose work he especially admires are David Brill, Kunihiko Kasahara, Stephen Weiss, and of course, the late Akira Yoshizawa. Continually refining his airplanes, the "Nike" with Display Stand was improved for publication in this book. He lives in Toronto.
www.origamitoronto.org

Chou Hung

A neuroscientist by day, paper airplane enthusiast by night, Dr. Hung resurrected a forgotten model, the Saber Tooth, and improved its superior flight characteristics. Hung lives in Taiwan.
www.geocities.com/chouhung/saber.html

Paul Jackson

From abstract, sculptural forms to origami animals and airplanes, Jackson's models highlight beauty and simplicity in design with paper as art. He has published dozens of titles, including easy-to-understand pop-up books, as well as other papercraft and paper airplane subjects. Jackson lives in Israel and is the founder of the Israeli Origami Center.
www.origami-artist.com

Kunihiko Kasahara

Perhaps the most prolific origami author ever—with over one hundred books—Kasahara's designs are inserted into nearly every packaged collection of origami paper. He has developed countless techniques and made discoveries, and he is revered by all who practice origami. The Hang Glider comes from his book **Origami Omnibus**. Kasahara lives in Japan.

Michael LaFosse

LaFosse is an extraordinary origami creator and paper airplane designer. First to develop the fuselage lock— the most significant advance in origami airplane design ever. He has written several dozen books, and has produced two paper airplane DVDs: **Planes for Brains** and **Aerogami**. Origamido makes the world's finest-quality handmade origami paper for discriminating creators. LaFosse lives in Hawaii.
www.origamido.com

Sipho Mabona

Mabona is an origami and paper airplane creator developing some of the newest, most radical designs. One of his designs placed second in the Red Bull Paper Wings International Competition, the world's leading paper airplane contest. Sipho lives in Switzerland.
www.flickr.com/photos/sipmab

Nick Robinson

Robinson has authored dozens of books, including **Super Simple Paper Airplanes**. He is a prolific origami creator and has pioneered many innovative techniques. Nick has a comprehensive Web site devoted to his origami work. Robinson lives in England.
www.nickrobinson.info/origami

James Sakoda

The late James M. Sakoda won the Origami category in the First International Paper Airplane Competition held in 1966 by **Scientific American**. He was a computer science professor in the Department of Sociology and Anthropology at Brown University in Providence, Rhode Island.

Alex Schultz

Schultz maintains a comprehensive Web site with lots of free paper airplanes, including video instructions for folding. There are links to a variety of paper airplane–related topics. Schultz lives in California.
www.paperairplanes.co.uk

Teong Hin Tan

Tan wanted to create better paper airplanes for his son, who launched his interest. Since he was already an aerospace engineer, he naturally developed 3-D, realistic-looking aircraft. And with his origami knowledge, he also developed an interlock that helps keep the plane's shape consistent in flight. Tan's book, **Interlocking and 3-D Paper Airplanes**, contains many more exciting models. He lives in Singapore.
www.trafford.com/robots/
04-1926.html
phone: 888-232-4444

Darren Thorne

At his Web site, Thorne has a package of very creative and beautifully patterned models in a PC-based program. His original designs are shown with easy-to-read instructions using clear photographs and diagrams. Print the stylized, custom layouts on any printer, then fold and fly. Thorne lives in California.
www.aerogami.com

Stephen Weiss

Striving for clean, efficient design and whimsy, Weiss designs his models to require little or no trim. He has written two origami books, including **Wings and Things: Origami That Flies**. A leading origami creator, his models have been exhibited throughout the world, including the Smithsonian Institution. Weiss lives in Miami Beach, Florida.

Allan and David Wise

Allan and his brother, David, invented their signature paper airplane Greatest YZ for their primary school playground competitions. According to Allan, one day, with favorable thermal updrafts, the undefeated "Wisey," as it was known, recorded a ten-minute flight from a standing start traveling more than 500 feet (150 meters)! The Wise brothers live in Australia.
www.draftsperson.net/origami

Makoto Yamaguchi

Gallery Origami House was founded in 1989 to foster talent and expression from all who love to fold paper. Yamaguchi has authored more than sixty books, most designed for children, his primary audience. His consistent use of clear, concise diagramming and clever illustrations give his books an unexpected design appeal as well. Yamaguchi lives in Japan.
www.origamihouse.jp

Thay Yang

Yang's books, **Exotic Airplanes** and **Exquisite Interceptors**, are definitely for the advanced enthusiast. At only eighteen years of age, he was a Senior Aesthetics award winner in the Great International Paper Airplane Contest, foreshadowing his worldwide recognition as a designer of realistic, precision-crafted paper airplanes. Yang lives in California.
www.cypresshouse.com
phone: 800-773-7782

Picture Reference

This quick guide shows each model, alphabetized by name. Some pictures show another view of the plane or one folded from an alternate patterned paper.

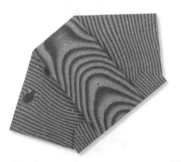

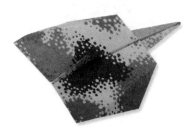

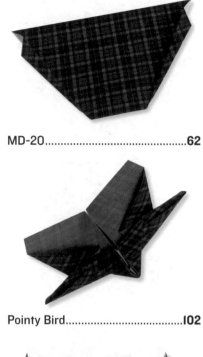

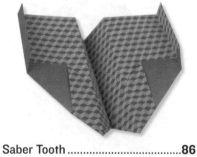

About the Author

LACOPPOLA-MEIER

Jeff Rutzky's report card in kindergarten stated that he "works well with paper and scissors." Paper crafts have been a passion throughout his life, and in his adulthood, he has integrated them with his desktop publishing and computer-controlled cutting skills to create unique works of art.

Jeff is also author and designer of several origami books and kits, including **Kirigami**, which features forty-seven exquisite paper art projects to fold and cut, from 3-D snowflakes and ornaments to pop-up cards and origamic architecture. Look for his titles at your local Barnes & Noble Booksellers or online at bn.com.

Jeff works as an author, graphic designer, and artist in New York City.